D1488876

Priestly Wisdom:

Insights from St. Benedict

by Rev. Mark O'Keefe, OSB

© 2004
Saint Meinrad School of Theology

ISBN 0-87029-389-3

Printed at Abbey Press
1 Hill Drive
St. Meinrad, IN 47577

Excerpts from *RB 1980: The Rule of St. Benedict in English*, © 1981, The Liturgical Press, Collegeville, Minnesota, used with permission. All rights reserved.

All rights reserved. No part of this publication may be reproduced, stored in a retrieval system, or transmitted in any form, or by any means—electronic, mechanical, photocopying, recording or otherwise—without the written permission of Saint Meinrad School of Theology.

Table of Contents

Acknowledgments

I want to express my thanks to those who helped me with the preparation of this, my fifth book of reflections on the priesthood. Most of the chapters began as conferences that I delivered to the seminarians at Saint Meinrad over the course of a couple of years. Some of them took on a slightly different form and content as I offered alternate versions during retreats for bishops and priests. In a few cases, retreat conferences made their way into rector's conferences. The reactions, questions and comments offered by these bishops, priests and seminarians have served to advance and sometimes revise my thinking; and I appreciate their input.

I want to thank my secretary, Mrs. Marilyn Brahm, for typing earlier drafts of many of these chapters from handwritten texts. This work, of course, is just one very, very small part of the immense assistance that she offers me on a regular basis.

Mrs. Mary Jeanne Schumacher, the director of communications at Saint Meinrad, once again ably assisted by Mrs. Jo Rita Bishop, offered editorial advice and skill to the preparation of this final text. Together, they guided it efficiently through the publication process.

My friend and colleague, Fr. Justin DuVall, OSB, the vice rector at Saint Meinrad, read the penultimate draft of the text. His comments have greatly improved my prose and my reflection on the *Rule of St. Benedict* (at least within the limitations of my prose style and my understanding of the depth and subtlety of the *Rule*). The seminarians say that Fr. Justin is a "monk's monk"—which is to say that the depth of his monastic identity, reflection and commitment is readily apparent to all. The seminarians are right.

Finally, I want to express my appreciation to my superior, Archabbot Lambert Reilly, OSB. Archabbot Lambert is one of the few people who claims to enjoy proofreading, but his assistance goes far beyond that somewhat-mundane task. As this book goes into publication, he prepares to step down as archabbot of Saint Meinrad, after nine years as its leader and guide. His accomplishments have been many. During these nine years, I have learned, however imperfectly, many things from him about leadership, about people and about the life of the Spirit. He has been unfailing in his support of the School of Theology in so many ways; he has been constant in his encouragement and solicitude toward me personally and in my role as rector; he has been a good friend to me. I respectfully and gratefully dedicate this book to Archabbot Lambert.

References and Abbreviations

The Second Vatican Council

DV	*Dei Verbum* (Constitution on Divine Revelation), 1965
LG	*Lumen Gentium* (Constitution on the Church), 1964
PO	*Presbyterorum Ordinis* (Decree on the Ministry and Life of Priests), 1965

Pope John Paul II

PDV	*Pastores Dabo Vobis* (I Will Give You Shepherds), 1992
Gift and Mystery	*Gift and Mystery: On the Fiftieth Anniversary of My Priestly Ordination*. New York: Doubleday, 1996

Congregation for the Clergy

Directory	*Directory for the Life and Ministry of Priests*, 1994
Priest	"The Priest: Teacher of the Word, Minister of the Sacraments, Leader of the Community." *Origins* 29 (September 9, 1999): 197-211.

Committee on Priestly Life and Ministry, National Conference of Catholic Bishops

FIYH	*Fulfilled in Your Hearing: The Homily in the Sunday Assembly*, 1982

St. Benedict

RB	*The Rule of St. Benedict (RB 1980: The Rule of St. Benedict in English)*. Collegeville: The Liturgical Press, 1982

Introduction

I am the president-rector of a seminary owned and operated by Benedictine monks primarily for the formation of diocesan priests. It seems like a bit of a paradox, doesn't it? What business do Benedictine monks have (even with the rich collaboration of diocesan priests, other religious and laity) in preparing men for the busy, outward-focused ministry and life of parish priests? Well, in my almost 20 years on our seminary faculty and staff, and especially in my last eight-and-a-half years as president-rector, I have had ample opportunity to ponder that apparent paradox.

Of course, at Saint Meinrad, part of the answer is simply historical. One hundred and fifty years ago, the Bishop of Vincennes, Indiana, (now the Archdiocese of Indianapolis) sent one of his priests to Europe, looking for German-speaking religious to establish a seminary to prepare a native clergy. He found at the Swiss Abbey of Einsiedeln a willing abbot, and so Benedictine monks came to southern Indiana to form priests for our country and, ultimately, beyond. In a sense, the historic Benedictine work of education and learning took on a particular focus to meet the needs of the Church at the time—seminary formation, marked by the Benedictine spirit, expressed in the School's motto *Sanctitate et Scientia* (Through Holiness and Learning).

But my musings have led me beyond the fact of mere necessity at a particular time in ecclesial history in the United States to ponder a contemporary response to this seeming paradox of monks preparing parish priests. I have had many conversations with my brother-monks on the seminary faculty and staff about their understanding of our shared history, our monastic community's commitment of so much of its resources to the work of priestly formation, and their own personal, usually lifelong, investment in this work. I have spoken with the diocesan priests, other religious and laity on our faculty and staff about how they understand this seemingly paradoxical enterprise they have joined. And I have spoken with our clerical and lay alumni about what it meant to them to be educated, formed, by monks in a Benedictine ethos.

These musings and many conversations over these last two decades have convinced me that—paradox or not—there is a distinctive value that Benedictine monks and a Benedictine spirit brings to the formation of diocesan priests. At one time, this conviction took the form almost of a defense—a kind of *apologia*—as a response to imagined (and sometimes not so imaginary) critics of our work. But what has become clear to me is that the testimony of our alumni, especially our diocesan priest alumni—what they *say* about the unique value of their priestly formation at Saint Meinrad, but especially the *lived* testimony of their lives and ministry as parish priests—quite simply attests to the value of the Benedictine spirit of the priestly formation at Saint Meinrad.

What are some of the elements of this distinctively Benedictine contribution to a holistic priestly formation?

• The monks, young and especially old, witness to lifelong commitment and to fidelity—to those who must make and keep lifelong commitments in a culture that often doubts the possibility and even the desirability of such commitments.

• The church bells that call the monks to Mass and to common prayer throughout the day give testimony to the importance of a faithful rhythm of prayer for oneself, for a community, and for the Church and world—to those who must be men of prayer and who must pray daily for and on behalf of the Church.

• The Benedictine monastic tradition and spirit manifests the importance of the liturgy and liturgical prayer, celebrated reverently, prayerfully, in a manner that calls people to worship—to those who must gather and lead the People of God at prayer, most especially at the Eucharist.

• At the same time, Benedictine spirituality focuses attention on the necessity of personal prayer, especially prayerful meditation on the Word of God (*lectio divina*)—to those whose first duty will be to proclaim and preach God's word to His people.

• A Benedictine monastic community gives testimony to the central importance of Christian community to the faithful living of the Christian faith—to those who must gather, nurture and lead Christian communities and who must enter wholeheartedly into the brotherhood of a diocesan presbyterate.

• In the Benedictine tradition, education is intimately linked with the pursuit of holiness (*Sanctitate et Scientia*—Through Holiness and Learning)—for those who are challenged, especially today, to embrace the necessity of an ongoing, lifelong, holistic formation as priests.

Many more important elements of the unique Benedictine contributions to priestly formation could be listed. Those are just a few, and others are contained in the subject matter of the chapters of this book.

From these musings about our work at Saint Meinrad, I have come to believe that St. Benedict—his *Rule* and the tradition he fathered—have important insights and lessons for priests who have no intention of becoming monks and who have no business taking on many of their distinctive monastic practices. And, thus, this book.

In each of the chapters that follow, I want to propose one broad aspect of St. Benedict's wisdom as it might apply to the life and ministry of priests, particularly parish priests. Although I have grouped the chapters together under broader themes, they can be read in any order. Reading and pondering the *Rule of St. Benedict* itself might further highlight my points, but I don't think it's necessary. Being formed for the priesthood at Saint Meinrad would certainly help (but, through no fault of their own, not every priest could be so fortunate). In the end, perhaps all that is necessary is an openness to learn from a master like St. Benedict, whose wisdom has guided so many monks and nuns—and priests and laity, too—for over 1,500 years.

Pastoring a Community

One

Insights on Leadership

Elegantly and vividly carved into the wooden door of the abbot's office at Saint Meinrad are the words of the Holy *Rule*: "He is believed to hold the place of Christ in the monastery" (RB 2:2). Perhaps there is no more striking way to suggest, in a Christian context, both the authority and the responsibility of a Benedictine abbot: "He is believed to hold the place of Christ in the monastery." This admonition of St. Benedict suggests that the leadership of the abbot is rooted deeply in a particular relationship with the Lord whose "place" he holds. And it suggests a strong sense of call, of vocation, in leadership. This distinct relationship with the Lord is the foundation of the abbot's call to leadership within the community.

I'd like to suggest that St. Benedict's teaching on the office of the abbot may have something to teach priests who are also called to "hold the place of Christ" in the Church, to make Christ present, to act in His name and in His person (to act *in persona Christi capitis*). The priest, too—most evident when he presides at the Eucharist—"holds the place of Christ" in the Church.

Of course, there are important differences between St. Benedict's abbot and a priest. In fact, it doesn't seem that Benedict assumed that the abbot had to be a priest, but I would like to suggest that there are lessons to be learned, nonetheless, from reflecting on what St. Benedict has to say about the leadership of the abbot.

St. Benedict's Images of the Abbot

I want to begin by looking at some of the images/metaphors that St. Benedict uses in describing the abbot and his leadership. Since the abbot is so strongly identified with Christ, most are images/metaphors that also have been used to describe the ministry of the Lord. They are images, therefore, that also can be used to describe the ministry of priests. Examining St. Benedict's use of these images for the abbot, then, may shed light on the leadership of priests.

Shepherd

Like Christ, the abbot, according to St. Benedict, is a *shepherd* (RB 2:6-10; 27:8-9). He is a shepherd/pastor of the monastic flock *and* of the individual monks (and *both* elements are important here). St. Benedict understood the monks to have set out on a common journey in response to God's call. In this sense, one commentator on the *Rule* has called the abbot a "pilgrimage leader" who continues to hold before the monks the "dream" that calls them always forward (Terence Kardong, OSB, *American Benedictine Review*, March 1991, 53-72). The goal is *both* the *individual* dream of fully attaining "that love which casts out fear" *and* the *communal* vision of "coming altogether into everlasting life."

On the journey, the abbot is to show toward the individual monks the solicitude of the Good Shepherd who was anxious to seek out the straying and the lost sheep, even carrying them on his own shoulders (RB 27:8-9). In doing so, the abbot has to move the flock forward without driving them so hard that the weak and the young fall behind.

St. Benedict's use of the image of shepherd, then, includes the more common idea of the pastoral care of individuals and flocks; but it also includes the important sense of leading a flock on a journey—fundamentally a spiritual journey (though, as we will see, a spiritual journey that cannot ignore the physical, the practical and the relational aspects of this shared pilgrimage).

Both elements of shepherding/pastoring are important: individual and communal, personal and institutional, spiritual and temporal—though many of us might prefer or might have more gifts for one than the other.

So, according to St. Benedict, the abbot is a shepherd or a pastor—as, of course, is a priest.

Steward

According to the *Rule*, the abbot is also a *steward* of both the spiritual and the material resources of the monastery (RB 64). He is an overseer, responsible to the Lord, for what he has been given and for what has been given to the community for its maintenance and growth. In fact, St. Benedict is quite emphatic that the abbot will be accountable to the Lord:

> Let the abbot always remember that at the fearful judgment of God, not only his teaching but also his disciples' obedience will come under scrutiny. The abbot must, therefore, be aware that the shepherd will bear the blame

> wherever the father of the household finds that the sheep have yielded no profit (RB 2:6-7).

And later, in the very same chapter (lest the abbot miss the point):

> The abbot must know that anyone undertaking the charge of souls must be ready to account for them. Whatever the number of brothers he has in his care, let him realize that on judgment day he will surely have to submit a reckoning to the Lord for all their souls—and indeed for his own as well. In this way, while always fearful of the future examination of the shepherd about the sheep entrusted to him and careful about the state of others' accounts, he becomes concerned also about his own, and while helping others to amend by his warnings, he achieves amendment of his own faults (RB 2:37-40).

Imagine if St. Benedict were issuing the same stern admonition to today's pastors, who also have undertaken "the charge of souls"!

The abbot exercises this stewardship directly in the decisions that he himself makes, but also through the careful appointments of other officials who will direct elements of the daily life of the community. Of course, being a good steward of even a small community—and even with good delegation—can take up a good deal of an abbot's attention (and temporal administration is obviously important); but St. Benedict is emphatic that material concerns must not make the abbot neglect his more basic spiritual stewardship of the community. The abbot's spiritual stewardship is to shape his temporal administration, rather than the reverse.

Father

Further, Benedict describes the abbot as a *father* (RB 2:24). Beyond merely insuring consistency with the tradition of desert fathers and mothers, this parental image allows Benedict to portray the abbot's leadership as fundamentally relational. He may be the "Lord and Abbot," as St. Benedict speaks of him at one point, but he is also a father to the monks and the community. The abbot is concerned for the good of the community because he is concerned for the good of its individual members. "Let him strive," says Benedict, "to be loved rather than feared" (RB 64:15).

Given Benedict's historical context, the father image also includes echoes of the Roman *paterfamilias*, the formidable father figure of a classic noble Roman household. This larger "family" unit included not only actual family members bonded by blood and close interpersonal ties, but also a whole complex of persons (managers, servants and slaves), duties, and physical and financial resources under the oversight of the powerful father of the household. St. Benedict's use of the image of father to describe the abbot, then, is able to embrace both the relational as well as the institutional aspects of this role.

Physician

In the "disciplinary" section of the *Rule*, the abbot is imaged as a *physician* (RB 28). He is to know how to "diagnose" the spiritual maladies of the individual monk and of the community, and he is to know how to apply the right remedy. This requires the essential abbatial characteristic of "discretion" (to be addressed in the next chapter).

This image of Christ and of the abbot as a physician provides an interesting and not-often-used metaphor for understanding priestly ministry. Perhaps we have thought of the pastor as a kind of "doctor of souls." Certainly, we have understood Jesus to be a "Divine Physician." There is a sense in which the priest must be skilled, wise and caring enough to understand the pastoral need of the individuals who come to him for help, whether in the confessional or in informal counseling situations. In this metaphorical sense, he must be able prudently to "diagnose" the issue (or help the person to do so) and suggest a remedy (or help the person to recognize one). Good preaching, as well, addressed to a particular community at a particular moment in its history, requires a similar kind of pastoral sensitivity in identifying what the parish needs to hear and how to address it effectively.

Teacher

Certainly, the predominant image of the Benedictine abbot is *teacher* (RB 2:11-15). This is consistent with Benedict's image of the monastery as a "school of the Lord's service" (RB Prol. 45).

While the abbot is to teach monastic "doctrine," he more fundamentally is a teacher of a *way of life*; and, while he is to teach by word, Benedict insists that he is to teach most especially by the example of his own life and actions (RB 2:11-12).

Further, while the abbot is conveying a teaching from the past, he must possess "a treasury of knowledge from which he can bring out what is old and new" (RB 64:9). The abbot is not just an encyclopedia of monastic information. No really good teacher is, after all, just a conveyor of information. The abbot must be wise and prudent to know what message needs to be heard by the community and by individual monks and what will speak to the needs of the moment.

The *Rule* has little to say about lectures or conferences given by the abbot to the monks. Much of his teaching is to be carried out through the actual exercise of his leadership: his example, his appointments, his decisions, and his interpretations of the demands of the tradition in response to the needs of the present.

Several years ago, Neely McCarter, a longtime president of a Protestant seminary, wrote a book titled *The President as Educator: A Study of the Seminary Presidency*. In a way, the book is meant to offer comfort to the many seminary presidents who left the classroom to take up seminary leadership. McCarter offers a word of encouragement to the seminary president that parallels the broad view of the teaching task of St. Benedict's abbot: although the president or the abbot might not teach in the classroom, he nonetheless teaches mightily by the decisions he makes, the institutional priorities he sets and the personal example of his life. He is an educator through the careful exercise of his leadership. While a contemporary priest may be a teacher in a more formal way, whether in RCIA or other parish adult education, this sense of the larger context of his teaching is important to keep in mind.

Lessons for Leadership

In speaking of the images of the abbot, I have already alluded to some aspects of St. Benedict's teaching that might shed light on priestly leadership and ministry, but I'd like to focus more explicitly on three particular lessons of St. Benedict's vision of leadership. First, St. Benedict makes clear that leadership that flows from a special relationship with Christ is a privilege (in the sense of being an awesome blessing), *and* it is a *responsibility*. Secondly, the teaching of a pastor must not only be *about* Christ; rather, it must *reveal* Christ and reveal the *way of life* that responds to Him. Thirdly, being a shepherd is a task that is, at once, both spiritual and temporal—neither can be neglected, but the abbot (like the priest) has to keep his priorities straight.

Blessing and Responsibility

"The abbot is believed to hold the place of Christ in the monastery."

To hold the place of Christ—to act in His name and His person as a priest does—is an awesome privilege and a tremendous responsibility, especially in the sense of being accountable to Christ whom one has been called to make present. St. Benedict says (RB 2:30), "The abbot must always remember what he is and remember what he is called, aware that more will be expected of a man to whom more has been entrusted." We might just as well say: "The *priest* must always remember what he is and remember what he is called." Priests are, as St. Benedict reminds the abbot, stewards—and stewards are accountable to their Lord.

But to hold the place of Christ, to make Him present, is a tremendous responsibility on us priests in another way: the responsibility of drawing always closer to Him, becoming more and more familiar with Him, knowing and loving Him ever more deeply, being conformed to Him ever more completely, becoming more transparently what ordination has made us.

To "hold the place of Christ" and "to make Him present" and "to act in His name and in His person" means the tremendous responsibility of living our lives so that we are not obstacles for others to see Him, to hear Him and, most fundamentally, to believe in Him. Rather, our lives must be transparent to Him so that phrases like "acting in His person" do not just bespeak our office, but identify our lives and ministry, our relationships and our ways of acting. Like St. John the Baptist, we must live the reality: "He must increase, while I must decrease."

Abbots and priests must teach by the way they live. They must model the way of life to which they call others. They must "hold the place of Christ" neither like an inert "seat reserved" sign nor like a foreign usurper, but as one in whom Christ can be recognized, even if always imperfectly.

Of course, in this life (marked as we are by sin), there always will be a disparity between the life of Jesus and our way of living and acting; but as Christians united to Him by baptism, and especially as priests specially configured to Him by ordination, we must strive to be able to say with St. Paul: "I live now, not I, but Christ lives in me"—not only in a spiritual and mystical sense, but as a manifest reality in life and in ministry.

Revealing Christ

A second lesson that St. Benedict's exhortations to the abbot can teach priests is that, because our ministry is rooted in a special relationship with Christ, our teaching must be not only *about* Christ ("right doctrine," as important as that is); it must be a teaching that *reveals* Christ and that helps others to live His *way of life*.

Right *understanding* about God is at the service of right *responding* to Him. Right *doctrine*, right *teaching*, right *understanding* must serve right *living* and right *loving* and right *ways of relating*—or that doctrine and teaching and understanding might as well stay on a printed page in a mildewy book in a seldom-used library.

Good preaching, the worthy celebration of the sacraments and effective teaching don't just tell others about Christ; they reveal *Him*; and they reveal the authentic way of responding to Him. In a similar way, increasingly over the course of his priestly life and ministry, the priest himself must reveal Christ in his ways of acting and relating. Although always imperfectly, in countless ordinary ways, he must be for the people an accurate reflection both of Christ as He relates to His people and of the authentic way in which the disciples of Christ must respond to Him. Just as Jesus was both the perfect revelation of the Father as well as the perfect revelation of the authentic human response to the Father's offer of love, so, too, the priest must reveal both Christ the True Pastor and the authentic way of responding to Him.

St. Benedict's abbot can't just teach doctrine; he must *reveal* Christ and teach a way of life that leads to Him. A priest, too, must reveal Christ in the various situations in which his people find themselves—revealing Him in special sacramental moments but revealing Him, too, in suffering, in loss and in disappointment, as well as in rejoicing and in celebration (even if "revealing" means, at the moment, standing there just "holding the place of Christ," being there "in His name").

St. Benedict's abbot teaches a way of life; and he does so by words; he does so by the decisions he makes; but he does so most especially by the way he lives the way of life to which he is calling others.

Both Spiritual and Temporal

A third lesson that we can draw from St. Benedict's wisdom about the abbot is that being a shepherd is a task that is, at once, both spiritual *and* temporal. Neither can be neglected, but the abbot (and the priest) has to keep his priorities straight. (A later chapter in this book is devoted to this topic, but I want to offer a briefer and slightly different reflection in this context.)

In speaking of the abbot as a shepherd, I alluded to the individual/pastoral/spiritual aspects, on the one hand, and to the community/institutional/temporal aspects of this responsibility, on the other hand. The abbot must be attentive to individuals even while he leads a community. He must be concerned about the spiritual and the temporal, the pastoral and the administrative. The abbot is a pastor of flesh-and-blood human beings with individual needs and weaknesses, strengths and talents; and, because they are flesh-and-blood, pastoring them also means being concerned for the community and its institutional needs.

Many priests hate administration. Some have little innate talent for it, less training to do it and even less inclination to seek out formal training for it. They wish someone else would do it and leave them free to do "real ministry"—by which I guess they would mean sacraments, preaching and one-to-one pastoral care. (Broader research, funded by the Lilly Endowment and sponsored by Saint Meinrad, confirms this analysis. See *The Reluctant Steward* [1992] and its follow-up, ten years later, *The Reluctant Steward Revisited* [2002].)

Regardless of their personal inclinations, St. Benedict suggests that the pastor (the abbot, the priest) must not neglect the institutional concerns even while he keeps a spiritual focus. For St. Benedict, the community life and order serve the spiritual good of the monks; if things are not ordered well, the spiritual good of the monks will suffer. A lot of the institutional details can be delegated to the other officials of the monastery, but the abbot must keep both oversight and active concern.

If a parish can afford lay administrators of the parish's practical needs, that's great; but a pastor must retain concern for those things. Otherwise, he's not really a pastor of flesh-and-blood people whose life together must be ordered well if their spiritual good is to be met.

You can be a great preacher; but if the microphones don't work or no one got around to buying them or turning them on, you're wasting your time. In fact, how could you be a great preacher, one Sunday after another, if you don't know the real needs, aspirations and situations of the people who make up your community? It's one thing to be a great mission preacher who can speak powerfully to common, general human spiritual experience in the various places that he preaches; it's another thing to preach to *this* community in its concrete situation and need. While being a traditional pastor is not the only vantage point from which to understand one's people, both in attitude and in experience, it is a unique perspective for preaching and ministry.

You might be a dynamic and prayerful presider at the sacraments; but if the church roof is leaking on the congregation or the boiler's not working in the winter or there's no one to address the conflict among the music ministers, your people might be a little too distracted to notice the awesome beauty of your presiding style. In fact, how can you really be a pastor of a community if you gather them at the Eucharist but have no concern, responsibility or practical knowledge of the community outside the Eucharist? It's one thing to be a sacramental minister; it's another thing to be a pastor. Again, being a true pastor is not the only perspective on the community; but it is a special one.

You might be a great advocate for the poor and alienated; but if you haven't begun to look ahead to ask how your parish is going to respond in welcome to immigrants, organize volunteers and hire ministers, or work with other parishes and organizations, your advocacy may be morally accurate but practically ineffective. Again, the person preaching doesn't have to be the one leading and managing the day-to-day effort, but the two have to work hand-in-hand.

The priest doesn't have to do all of these things himself—as St. Benedict says, delegation and collaboration are important skills—but if all the priest is concerned about is his preaching, his sacramental presiding and his one-to-one ministry, then the true spiritual good of his people is going to suffer for his lack of concern for institutional, administrative, managerial details that insure that their spiritual needs can be met.

Personally, I *feel* a lot more like a pastor when I preside at our community's special events or speak with a student about his vocation and discernment, but I *believe* that I am just as much a pastor when I am out raising money so that we can have a more worthy space in which our community's special events can be celebrated or so that we can afford more or better resources to aid in the seminarians' discernment and formation.

We all like to "play to our strengths" (and our interests). Many of us don't have much talent, interest or training in administration; and we'd rather do what is more obviously ministerial or pastoral. But, obvious or not, the good order of the community is a real ministerial and pastoral concern, a leader's concern.

St. Benedict's teaching about the abbot forewarns us that the role of the shepherd includes *both* spiritual and temporal matters, but it also teaches us that we have to keep the priorities straight: Temporal things must be ordered so that the spiritual good of the community is served; the temporal serves the spiritual and not the other way around. Bricks-and-mortar cannot take priority over pastoral care; meetings cannot take priority over set times for homily preparation; the best of plans cannot ignore the spiritual needs and personal sensitivities of the people involved. We cannot ignore the temporal and administrative, but we have to keep the priorities straight.

A Final Word About Prayer

"Keeping the priorities straight" must be a pastor's concern for his community and for the priorities of his leadership, but it must also be a concern for his own life as well.

Pastoral ministry is what we are about, but if we neglect our personal prayer, we are in danger of getting all of the priorities mixed up, in our ministry and in our personal life. Again, we must remember that we are stewards: it's the *Lord's* flock; they are the *Lord's* sheep; ultimately, *He* can take care of them. We, for our part, as flesh-and-blood sinners, need prayer.

Our pastoral ministry is about "holding *His* place," and so, our ministry is most authentic and most effective when He shines through it—and we don't get in the way of it. But that can happen only if we are faithful to our prayer. Otherwise, we will forget these three lessons of St. Benedict's wisdom: we will fail to live up to the responsibility that comes with the blessing of our special calling; we will find ourselves teaching important things *about* Christ but without *revealing* Him and the way of life that responds to Him authentically; and we will neglect important aspects of our ministry, spiritual or temporal, and find our personal and institutional priorities askew.

Two

Discretion

The priest is a leader. Today, he is often the leader of a complex parish organization, and this task requires that he possess an ability to delegate and to collaborate, certain basic managerial and financial skills, as well as skills for organizing, motivating and even fund-raising. But, beyond or perhaps more fundamental than these native gifts and learned skills, priestly leadership requires a particular virtue: priestly or pastoral prudence.

Prudence, according to St. Thomas, is the habitual disposition to decide and to choose well, the abiding inclination and ability to move from general principles to their application in sometimes-complex situations. Prudence, then, can be called "wisdom reduced to practice."

Prudence is a virtue at the level of personal decision-making, but Aquinas spoke, too, of "political prudence." The leader must be able to decide well for the sake of the common good, which is distinct from decision-making about his personal good. At the secular level, St. Thomas speaks of the "art of ruling well." The leaders of the Church community need such prudence as well—a prudence that can be called priestly or pastoral prudence.

St. Benedict on Discretion

St. Benedict was very concerned about the qualities that an abbot, as the leader of the monastic community, should possess.

One of the most important of these qualities is "discretion, the mother of virtues" (RB 64:19). Discretion is a virtue that embraces both what we would call the virtue of prudence as well as a spirit of discernment. Church leaders would do well to read St. Benedict's treatment of the abbot, especially in Chapters 2 and 64 of the *Rule*, where it becomes apparent how central he believed this virtue to be.

In Chapter 64, Benedict addresses the election of the abbot. He says that the man to be chosen must possess two fundamental characteristics: "wisdom in teaching" and "goodness of life" (RB 64:2). The connection of these two qualities manifests St. Benedict's emphasis on the abbot as a teacher of a way of life—importantly by the witness of his own way of living. But the abbot's "wisdom in teaching" extends beyond explicitly passing on the principles of the monastic tradition, whether in word or in action. As I mentioned in the previous chapter, St. Benedict says almost nothing about the abbot's preaching, giving conferences or formal teaching. "Wisdom in teaching" is expressed in such things as the appointment of other monastic officials, the decisions he makes, his priorities and his manner of dealing with the monks. The abbot's "wisdom in teaching" is therefore expressed in the discretion with which he exercises his leadership. In St. Thomas' terms, the abbot must be able to "reduce wisdom to practice."

As one reads the description of the abbot, it becomes clear that discretion involves the ability to make prudent decisions for the good of the community and for the good of its individual members in the practical realities of daily living.

The wisdom of the monastic tradition must always be lived in the actual reality of human existence. And so, in several places in his *Rule*, St. Benedict lays out regulations for such disparate and sometimes-minute matters as how the psalms are to be distributed in the daily common prayer, the number and character of meals during different seasons of the year, what the monks are to do when they are on a journey. But these sections often conclude with a statement like, "But, of course, if it seems good to the abbot to arrange it differently, he should do so." Again, we are reminded of the definition of prudence as wisdom reduced to practice.

But St. Benedict's description of discretion in various places is not simply about making appropriate practical decisions. St. Benedict admonishes the abbot that, in his decisions and actions, with all of the many temporal concerns of his office, he must remember that all are enjoined to "seek first the Kingdom of God and His justice." All of these very practical decisions must be approached with a "spiritual eye"—that is, with a recollection that all of those practical, temporal, administrative decisions have a spiritual purpose.

Surely, this is an important reminder for priests as well. Decisions in and for a parish can be so easily reduced to the practical, the temporal, the financial, the exclusively secular elements. Though such factors have a central place, good pastoral decisions for the good of the People of God must not neglect their broader and deeper spiritual purposes.

The teaching of St. Thomas Aquinas may help to shed further light on prudence at the service of spiritual ends. According to Aquinas, prudence, like all of the virtues, can be acquired by practice and consistent repetition. Prudence thereby becomes habitually operative in daily decision-making, resulting in effective and morally appropriate decisions. But every virtue, prudence included, according to St. Thomas, is also *infused* by grace, given by God as a gift (though obviously grace and our own efforts are meant to work together). The infused virtue of prudence empowers the individual in a new way through the action of grace. But the infused virtue does something more; it directs the natural virtue and its operation to a supernatural end. In short, what constitutes a truly good action is no longer simply the human, rational aspects but also their relationship to God and our relationship with Him.

It appears that both St. Benedict's teaching on the necessary abbatial virtue of discretion as well as our discussion of pastoral prudence include what St. Thomas would see as infused prudence. The abbot's discretion and the pastor's pastoral prudence enable them not to get lost in the merely or solely temporal and practical. Rather, abbot and pastor must be able to view and to address these things squarely, but in light of the spiritual purposes that the practical, administrative and temporal are meant to serve. Without this broader and deeper spiritual vision, decisions are restricted to important, but insufficient, temporal perspectives. In the service of God and the Church, the best decisions always encompass the rational and the practical but sometimes call for bold strides in faith and trust.

Of course, because infused virtues are given with grace, growth in these virtues requires a consistent openness to the workings of the Spirit. In short, the abbot grows authentically in the depth and breadth of discretion—and the priest, in pastoral prudence—not only with practice, but with prayer and sacraments, as well as the varied ways in which we encounter grace each day if we remain open.

Taking Counsel

In speaking of the abbot's decision-making, St. Benedict offers the abbot some very useful and practical advice: Always take counsel.

On the one hand, St. Benedict says that the monks ought to regard their leader as "Lord and Abbot," and, even today, an abbot's authority is quite extensive. But, at the same time, St. Benedict devotes the third chapter of the *Rule* to "Calling the Brethren to Counsel." There, he quotes the Book of Sirach (32:34): "Do everything with counsel and you will not be sorry afterward."

It's good practical advice about good decision-making: consult with others, and you'll get better information, perspectives and "buy-in"; but a closer look at St. Benedict's admonition to take counsel makes it clear that he is really talking about *discernment*.

In the chapter on summoning the brothers for counsel, St. Benedict says that all of the monks, including the youngest, should be consulted: "The reason why we have said all should be called for counsel is that the Lord often reveals what is better to the younger." (St. Benedict is apparently recalling the various Old Testament stories in which God chooses and speaks through the younger, for example, Joseph and David.)

We see that St. Benedict is not just offering practical advice: more counsel equals more information; more perspectives equal better "buy-in." Rather, he is reminding the abbot that his decision-making aims to be a discernment of God's will. Taking counsel is one way of finding out what God wants, assuming that the Lord speaks through the community and sometimes even through the youngest.

Truly good decisions cannot simply be the result of the widest consideration of human perspectives. Rather, they must be referred to the divine will and to spiritual purposes. Good decisions are the result of broad and deep listening—listening to what God wants, through the various avenues by which God speaks.

The abbot is being challenged to use, not just good common sense, but a spiritual sense—in short, discernment.

Too often in the daily lives of Christians, many of us try to make good decisions through collecting adequate information, investigating options, pondering consequences, getting advice, etc. Sadly, just as many of us seem to assume that God doesn't really speak a particular word or message to us as individuals in the Scriptures; in the same way, we often seem to assume that His will doesn't extend to the relatively minor, practical, administrative decisions we have to make. St. Benedict suggests otherwise: the abbot makes good decisions when he listens—to his monks, but, ultimately and particularly, through them to the Lord.

Discretion and Love

St. Benedict's admonition to discretion also extends to the abbot's ability to "size up" the monks and their individual needs and gifts. The abbot, the *Rule* says, must know how to challenge the strong to greater advances in their spiritual journey, but he also must know how to support the weak (RB 64:17-18). He must recall that some of the monks are like "bruised reeds," which he must not crush, or like already worn vessels that he must not break by scrubbing too hard. In sum, St. Benedict says (RB 64:17-19):

> ...he should be discerning and moderate, bearing in mind the discretion of holy Jacob, who said "If I drive my flocks too hard, they will all die in a single day (Gen. 33:13)." Therefore, drawing on this and other examples of discretion, the mother of virtues, he must so arrange everything that the strong have something to yearn for and the weak nothing to run from.

At one level, what St. Benedict is describing seems like simple shrewdness in dealing with people. But, given what he has said earlier in the *Rule* about the abbot's paternal and pastoral care of the monks, I suspect what he is saying is that this kind of ability to size up the needs of the individual monks is grounded in his care and solicitude for them. The abbot who holds the place of Christ in the monastery must attend to each of the monks as Christ would. Institutional concerns are important, but they are no excuse for ignoring or running roughshod over the particular needs of individual monks.

St. Thomas taught that charity is "the form of the virtues." Love is meant to fill all of the other virtues, empower them, integrate them and direct them to God. The abbot's love for the Lord and his pastoral love for his monks are meant to be "the form" of the virtue of discretion.

For the abbot and for the priest, pastoral love is meant to fill, empower and redirect discretion or pastoral prudence so that "good" decisions never simply leave the individual or certain groups behind. Perhaps in parish communities, the priest's pastoral love for the flock challenges him especially to consider the marginalized in his decision-making, whether their marginalization is because of economic status; racial, cultural or linguistic differences; differing ecclesial views; or newness to the parish.

Prudence's Enemy

In my book, *Priestly Virtues*, I offer a more general reflection on prudence. One of my most interesting discoveries in preparing that chapter was St. Thomas' discussion of the "enemy of prudence."

The enemy of prudence, according to Aquinas, is covetousness. The person who covets, who grasps after things selfishly, cannot make a truly prudent decision. Just when he should be taking into account the whole picture, self-interest and self-serving get in the way.

By covetousness, Aquinas means more than grasping after material possessions. It also includes coveting such things as status, human respect or power. When someone has an underlying priority to protect, promote or serve self, that person can't really make a prudent decision.

And when a person in authority is afflicted with a spirit of covetousness—whether for material things or more intangible possessions like status or power—that person can't make prudent decisions for others and for the common good.

I believe that our reflection on pastoral love and prudence suggests that the antidote, the remedy, for covetousness is a pastoral love for the flock. When a pastor loves his people, when he is willing to "lay down his life for the flock," when their needs take priority over his wants or selfish desires, he is free to make truly prudent decisions on their behalf. Such decisions may make his life harder or cause consternation to some, but they are the best decisions for all.

Sometimes, then, pastoral prudence requires fortitude, because some decisions will not be met with human favor. If the decisions are made with the good of others in mind, rather than his own, a pastor (whether abbot or priest) stands ready to make such decisions.

Tradition and Change

A final aspect of St. Benedict's teaching on discretion to which I want to refer is the abbot's responsibility to hold together tradition and change.

St. Benedict sees that the abbot must know how to adapt the rules to new circumstances and to the particular needs of the community at a particular time. On the one hand, the abbot must faithfully hand on the monastic tradition, the learned wisdom of those who have gone before, the proven way of life by which many have gone to God. But, at the same time, the abbot can be called a "pilgrimage leader." The monastic community and its monks are on a journey, and the terrain is always changing. The abbot must not get bogged down in "the way that it has always been done." Rather, standing firmly on and within a tradition, he must constantly be looking ahead to where the Lord is directing him and the community. Again, wisdom reduced to practice.

Conclusion

Discretion, says St. Benedict, is the mother of virtues. The exercise of every virtue, says St. Thomas, must be guided by prudence. Whether exercised by an abbot or a priest, the ministry of leadership in the Church, following the model of Jesus, is directed to the good of others over self; it attends to others in their uniqueness and in their particular needs; it cherishes others even as it challenges them; and, while it steadfastly upholds traditions and principles, it knows how these apply (and sometimes don't apply) in actual, often-complex situations with real flesh-and-blood people. God help the Christian community led by someone without the virtue of discretion!

Three

Hospitality

Benedictines are known for hospitality, and this charism of welcome finds its roots firmly in the *Rule of St. Benedict* itself. Of course, hospitality has never been the exclusive virtue of monks, but I'd like to suggest that what St. Benedict has to say about welcoming others can offer some important insights about how priests might understand their own ministry, especially as leaders of parish communities.

St. Benedict on Hospitality

Chapter 53 of the *Rule of St. Benedict* begins with these words: "All guests who present themselves are to be welcomed as Christ, for he himself will say 'I was a stranger and you welcomed me' (Matt. 25:35)." A few verses later (RB 53:6), Benedict adds: "All humility should be shown in addressing a guest on arrival or departure. By a bow of the head or by a complete prostration of the body, Christ is to be adored because he is indeed welcomed in them." And still later in the same chapter (RB 53:15): "Great care and concern are to be shown in receiving poor people and pilgrims, because in them more particularly Christ is received; our very awe of the rich guarantees them special respect."

St. Benedict goes on in some detail to talk about washing the guests' hands and feet, praying and sharing Scripture with them, offering them a meal and insuring them adequate bedding. Even the usual fasts and rules of silence bend in order to make the guest feel welcome. But, of course, what, after all, is the purpose of the silence, the fasts, the rules but to prepare the monk to welcome Christ, however Christ might choose to come…and in this case, in the guest?

The key element, then, of St. Benedict's "theology" of hospitality is that true hospitality involves welcoming the other person as Christ. Interpreting the judgment scene from the Gospel of Matthew almost literally, Benedict taught that, in welcoming other people, the monks are welcoming Christ himself. Two famous stories in the lives of monastic saints illustrate the teaching of St. Benedict.

St. Martin of Tours, before he became a monk and later a bishop, was a Roman soldier in Gaul in the fourth century. His legend tells us that, on a cold winter night, he encountered a shivering and half-naked beggar in danger of freezing to death. Filled with compassion, Martin cut his own warm military cloak in half and gave half to the poor man. Later that night, Jesus appeared to Martin, wearing the part of the cloak that Martin had given to the stranger. St. Martin had clothed Christ in need without knowing it (or even directly intending it).

A similar story is recounted about Pope St. Gregory the Great in the late sixth century. As pope, Gregory showed great concern for the poor of Rome and would welcome them into his own home for meals. One day, among his impoverished guests, Gregory encountered Jesus clothed as a beggar. St. Gregory had been feeding Christ in his solicitude for his unfortunate brothers and sisters.

And so, before there were hotels and inns for travelers and pilgrims, there were monasteries that followed St. Benedict's teaching, welcoming the rich and poor alike. And these monasteries offered more than a welcome to refresh the body; they also offered a welcome to refresh the spirit. Each guest was to be offered, not just food and a bed and a bath, but shared prayer and a shared breaking open of God's word.

The Witness of Christian Faith

Of course, the importance of hospitality was not new to St. Benedict. It had deep roots in the Jewish, Christian and monastic traditions. Recall in the Book of Genesis (18) the story of Abraham and Sarah welcoming the three strangers with elaborate hospitality: bows and foot-washing and a fine meal. Were they angels or the Lord Himself? The text seems to blur the two. But it is undoubtedly this text that the author of the Letter to the Hebrews had in mind when he said (Heb. 13:2): "Do not neglect hospitality, for through it, some have unknowingly entertained angels."

There are many other such stories of God—or of God's messengers—coming in the form of strangers: the story of Sodom and Gomorrah whose offense is popularly interpreted as grave sexual misconduct but is more likely gravely inhospitable offenses against the strangers; there is the angel who wrestled unidentified with Jacob; the stranger who came to Gideon in the Book of Judges to call him to lead the people against the Midianites; the companion of young Tobias in the Book of Tobit. God comes to His people in mysterious ways, in unlikely characters and circumstances (and *to* unlikely characters *in* unlikely circumstances), and His people need to stand ready to offer Him welcome.

But the people of Israel had additional reason to be hospitable toward strangers. They themselves had been wanderers and strangers after the great Exodus and aliens in diaspora after the great Exiles.

In the Gospel, we sometimes see the importance of hospitality through its failure to be offered. This is the case when Jesus rebukes Simon the Pharisee. Simon had failed to offer the customary signs of welcome: the washing of feet and the anointing. Instead, the poor sinful woman washes the feet of the Lord with her tears. In that story—as in a number of others—Jesus the Guest becomes Jesus the Host (cf. Rev. 3:20). The guest in the house of Simon becomes a true host to this woman—showing hospitality to the sinner—and showing the disciples what true hospitality means.

In the Gospel accounts, we can see the scope of the hospitality offered by Jesus: to sinners, to lepers, to the outcast, to hated Samaritans and Gentiles. And, with eyes of faith, we see Jesus as the gracious host of the Last Supper in which He shares His Body and Blood with sinners. And now, that hospitality is offered anew at each and every celebration of the Eucharist through the ministry of the priest.

Jesus offers hospitality to sinners, and so these welcomed sinners must themselves offer hospitality to others. Nowhere is this fact more clearly portrayed than in the text that became so important for St. Benedict. In the judgment scene in the Gospel of Matthew, we see the central importance of welcoming the Lord in the poor, the sick, the imprisoned and the stranger: "I was a stranger and you welcomed me" (Mt. 25:35). St. Benedict's invitation, then, to welcome others as Christ is really a fundamental lesson for all Christians and simply his explication of a Gospel command.

Welcoming Others as Gift

Several years ago, Irish moral theologian Enda McDonagh (*Gift and Call*, 1975) asked the question: "Where does the sense of moral obligation come from?" Why do we feel that we ought to do anything? In response, McDonagh suggests that this sense of moral obligation is rooted in an intuitive, pre-cognitive sense of the uniqueness of another human being—that is, the other person as gift: unique and irreplaceable, precious and sacred. We therefore feel intuitively that we ought to act in certain ways toward other persons—and refrain from acting in other ways. Moral obligation, then, is rooted in the giftedness of others.

Unfortunately, our personal sin and selfishness, as well as the darkness that sin casts on our relationships in society, blinds us to this fundamental intuition. It is faith that fully reveals the true giftedness of other persons: each person created in the image of God, held in existence and loved individually by God at every moment, redeemed by Christ in the humanity that Christ shared with them and in which He identified Himself with them.

Both nature and faith teach us, then, what St. Benedict taught in his *Rule*: we must welcome others as images of God, as sons and daughters of God, as brothers and sisters in Christ, and as Christ Himself.

Hospitality Begins at Home

The importance of such hospitality toward others is, of course, not only for strangers and guests. It is for the people around us; because, though it is true that we sometimes favor the people we know, it is nonetheless also true that we are sometimes better to guests and strangers than to the people with whom we live and work with each day. There is an old saying, "Charity begins at home." Perhaps we could say equally, "Hospitality begins at home; that is, with the people with whom we live and work."

The importance of this truth was not lost on St. Benedict, who also challenged his monks to treat one another as Christ, most especially the poor, the sick, the elderly and the young.

Although without taking the time to develop the thought fully in this context, I would suggest that chastity can also be understood through the lens of hospitality. Chastity is about welcoming persons as unique gifts rather than as collections of attractive body parts, as unique children of God rather than as potential objects for selfish pleasure.

A Priestly Hospitality

St. Benedict's admonition to welcome others as Christ is important to all of us, as disciples of Jesus and as a community of His followers. But it is also a special value for priests and a lens through which priests can view their daily ministry.

People who come to visit our seminary at Saint Meinrad often comment on the hospitality that they experience from the seminarians. I hope—and I believe—that this is so. Such a spirit of ready welcome is an extension of our Benedictine hospitality, but I believe firmly that it is also a lesson that seminarians are learning precisely in preparation for priestly ministry. Lessons practiced in greeting guests in the corridor, in giving directions to lost visitors, in serving at receptions and banquets are already forming a future attitude toward ministry and toward those encountered in ministry.

Catholic parishes must be places and communities of welcome; the Eucharist must be a celebration that invites and welcomes all people; and a pastor must be one who nurtures a spirit of welcome in the community and its staff. Of course, he must offer welcome to new parishioners and guests; but he must also offer a broader and more fundamental welcome to the People of God who come for worship and prayer, for guidance and support in times of trial, and for reconciliation in times of alienation.

What I am suggesting is that the hospitality of the priest is not simply the welcome offered at the beginning of Mass or when new parishioners come to the parish office to register. It is an attitude of ministry—i.e., a virtue that should mark the life and ministry of the priest.

Ministry is about hospitality. In whatever form or context, ministry involves welcoming others as they are and in their concrete and unique circumstances, welcoming Christ in them, and, then, helping them to see and to welcome Christ for themselves in the sometimes-unlikely situations where He is not easily recognized.

As others have said, priestly ministry is often a ministry carried out through the interruptions—that is, in the midst of what *seem* like interruptions: the person in danger of death at the hospital when I just settled down to watch the news, the parishioner who stops me after Mass when I'm on the way to the next thing on my daily calendar, the person whom I don't like who always has a question or a suggestion or a veiled criticism who now wants to talk about some problem.

Of course, the guest in a Benedictine monastery is, in many ways, also an interruption—an interruption to an ordered life, a rule of silence, and a schedule of prayer and work. But Christ comes to us in sometimes-surprising ways, doesn't He? Shall we take the chance of passing Him by—He who said, "I was naked or sick or imprisoned or a stranger and you attended to me"?

An attitude of hospitality in priestly ministry relates also to the utter importance of simple kindness in the daily exercise of that ministry. How easy it is for priests to alienate, hurt or make people feel dismissed with a simple unkind word or a look of annoyance! No priest has perfect patience; we have important tasks to which we must attend; on a human level, we are entitled to our moods; but we have to be vigilant of our power to hurt others, especially at vulnerable times, through the inhospitality of unkindness.

A More Basic, Prior Hospitality

Thus far, I have been reflecting on *our* hospitality; but, of course, there is a more basic hospitality, a prior hospitality: the hospitality that God offers to us—that is, to creatures and to sinners.

We hear the echo of this divine hospitality when we hear Jesus say (John 14:2-3), "In my father's house, there are many dwelling places. If there were not, would I have told you that I am going to prepare a place for you? And if I go and prepare a place for you, I will come back again and take you to myself, so that where I am going you also may be."

A "dwelling place" in the Father's house! But, of course, it is not simply a welcome to a "place." It is a welcome into the very heart of God! Jesus has gone ahead to prepare a welcome into the very life and the love of Father, Son, Spirit.

What greater hospitality and what greater incentive to hospitality: God welcomes sinners into His own divine life, into His heart, into His "house"—in "heaven," in the life to come, but also, if imperfectly and incompletely, in this life through our communion with Him. Again, at every celebration of the Eucharist, Christ welcomes His brothers and sisters in the person of the priest to a foretaste of the Heavenly Banquet where He feeds His people with a share in the Divine Life.

Obviously, the Church is not heaven. It is not the inner life of God. But it is its herald. It should be its witness. Through its sacramental life, it offers the foretaste of welcome that awaits us. And so, the Church must be a community of welcome—of welcome to sinners, of welcome to all.

Welcome offered by whom? Why, by all its members, but most especially by the Church's pastors! The one who stands in the place of Christ as Pastor (*in persona Christi capitis*)—that is, the priest—must be the chief minister of welcome, the leading minister of hospitality. Through him, it will be Christ who truly welcomes.

Looking again at Chapter 53 (vs. 14) of the *Rule*, St. Benedict tells the monks that, after they wash the feet of the guests, they are to recite the verse from Psalm 48 (vs. 10): "God, we have received your mercy in the midst of your temple." In a way, it seems like an odd thing to do and to say at that moment. Why that text? It seems to me that it recalls that those who are now welcoming others have themselves been welcomed by God, have themselves received His mercy. At the same time, it reminds them that the monastery into which they are welcoming their guests is really God's Temple: they are its stewards, not its owners.

So, too, with pastors who have themselves been welcomed by Christ into His Church even as they now welcome others—welcoming others into the parish and the liturgy that is not theirs but Christ's. As priests, we must be ministers of God's hospitality to sinners: to the people we don't like, who come at inconvenient moments, who disagree with us, who irritate us, who are alienated from the Church, who are in no way attractive or advantageous to us.

Hospitality to God

And as God offers hospitality, we, in turn, must offer hospitality to God.

In the Gospel of John (15:23), Jesus says, "Whoever loves me will keep my word, and my Father will love him, and we will come to him and make our dwelling with him." God will make His dwelling in the hearts of sinners! "Behold, I stand at the door and knock!"

Do we need any greater incentive to be people of prayer! For, what is prayer but hospitality offered to the ever-present God?

The spirit that is able consistently to stand ready to welcome Christ in every person is really a spirit that regularly welcomes Him in prayer. The one who has welcomed Christ into his own heart—who has prepared a dwelling for Him in regular solitude, in silence, and in prayer—is the one who stands ready to welcome Him in others. The person who, in prayer, has been able to see the Lord present, even in the sometimes-unlikely events of his life, has better vision to see Him present in the sometimes-unlikely people who interrupt his day. The person who celebrates the giftedness of his own life in prayer is better prepared to welcome the giftedness of others. The one who marvels in thanks and adoration at the gracious hospitality of God is more disposed to be hospitable to others.

Prayer opens our eyes to Christ in others: Prayer of *intercession* makes us sensitive to the needs of others. Prayer of *repentance* makes us aware of the ways that we alienate and marginalize others. Prayer of *gratitude* readies us to rejoice in the unique giftedness of those who come into our lives. Prayer of *adoration* reminds us to share the unimaginable hospitality of God, who invites us to dwell with Him and who comes to dwell in us in the deepest communion.

Perhaps this is another reason that hospitality is a special (though not exclusive) charism of monks. The daily prayers of a praying community, made up of monks who struggle every day to welcome one other as Christ, prepare the monks to welcome Him in those who come to them.

It is prayer that makes true hospitality possible; and so, St. Benedict is anxious that, even in welcoming guests, the basic rhythm of life and the silence be maintained by the monastic community. (And so, there is a tension between welcoming with open arms and still remaining true to prayer and work.)

This, too, it seems to me, is a lesson for priests: A hospitable ministry must be nourished by prayer; otherwise, all of the activity easily becomes just a matter of more programs, services and activities rather than being about people. And without prayer, the priest is in danger of burnout, because the demands of a hospitable ministry never end.

The virtue of hospitality is not the private charism of Benedictine monks. But I do think that St. Benedict has something distinctive to teach us about a hospitable and a prayerful ministry, a ministry that welcomes Christ and that invites others into the life of Christ. St. Benedict's wisdom tells us, I believe, that priestly ministry must be a ministry of hospitality—toward God and toward other people!

Living in the Tension

Four

Spiritual and Temporal

A contemporary Benedictine abbot often leads a complex and demanding life. He must live in an unavoidable tension. On the one hand, he is a pastor, a spiritual teacher and a father to his monks. On the other hand, depending on the size and complexity of the monastery and its apostolates, he is also an administrator, a manager and a development officer. Both in his personal life and in the focus of his leadership, the abbot must try to find a balance, maintaining his own life of prayer amidst many and varied activities and never losing sight of the spiritual, pastoral needs of the monks, even as he oversees the community's temporal needs.

I imagine that it can be quite a balancing act. And I assume that it is not entirely unlike the balancing act that contemporary priests must often strive to maintain in their own lives and ministry. St. Benedict's wisdom in addressing his abbot may, therefore, again have valuable insights to offer today's priests.

A Bit of History

It appears that the office of abbot can be traced back to the spiritual parenthood of desert fathers and mothers (*abbas* and *ammas*) in the deserts of Egypt and Syria in the third and fourth centuries.

The spiritual father or mother passed on the wisdom of the desert "way" and tradition, that is, the received monastic "doctrine." And the *abba* or *amma* provided prudent guidance in the disciple's search for God, based on the received wisdom as well as his or her own experience and prayer.

These earliest monastic leaders had no particular administrative leadership roles, but very soon some of the desert searchers began to live together as small groups. And soon thereafter, these loosely organized groups gave way to large and complex communities of vowed monks, requiring not only spiritual guidance but also effective administration of more institutionalized communities.

Writing in the sixth century, St. Benedict was very much aware that the leader of his community, the abbot, would somehow have to combine two roles: on the one hand, spiritual teacher and father, shepherd and pastor; and, on the other hand, leader, manager and overseer of a stable institution.

Of course, it appears that St. Benedict was practical and experienced; and so, one of his first responses was *delegation*. He called for the appointment of a prior to assist him in the oversight of the entire community, deans to oversee smaller groupings within the community, a manager of the temporal goods of the monastery, someone to oversee directly the formation of new members, etc. (It is interesting to note, in this context, that St. Benedict exhorts the cellarer, who manages the monastery's temporal goods, to "regard all utensils and goods of the monastery as sacred vessels of the altar" [RB 31:10]. In the monastery, the temporal and the sacred are always intimately linked.)

But, at the same time, St. Benedict realized that the tension between the spiritual and administrative roles of the abbot could not be resolved simply by delegation. Often, not everything can be delegated; and attending to these essential tasks and overseeing the delegates could easily fill one's time.

For the abbot to maintain a healthy and authentic balance in his spiritual and temporal tasks, according to Benedict, he must consistently remember that the essential work of temporal administration must be understood, not as separate from his shepherding and spiritual fatherhood, but rather as part of it. The spiritual good of the monks requires the good practical order of the community; and, therefore, the abbot's spiritual leadership necessarily involves a concern for the often-mundane practicalities of the common life.

As I mentioned in a previous chapter, I believe that this can be an important insight and reminder for priests. Some, perhaps many, priests feel that meetings, administration and various other practicalities are simply distractions from the "real" ministry of pastoring. Or those, perhaps few, priests who actually enjoy administration may feel guilty that they get energized by the details of a building project, fund-raising or parish plant when they "ought" to find their energy only in more "pastoral" things. But it seems to me—both from my reading of St. Benedict's wisdom and my own experience as a seminary pastor and administrator—administration is really an aspect of pastoring flesh-and-blood people in a human institution. How could it be otherwise?

I don't mean to suggest, by any means, that a priest-pastor shouldn't delegate or find qualified people to do what he can't, but there is simply no way that consistent effective pastoral care, ministry and parish outreach can happen without effective administration.

A priest is ordained to stand in the place of Christ as Shepherd and Pastor, but he is a shepherd and pastor not only of souls, but of *embodied* souls in community. A priest without such concern for and, at some level, oversight of the temporal good of that community is not a pastor in its broadest sense. Pastoral necessity may require priests to be sacramental ministers to parishes overseen by lay people, religious or deacons, but even the best sacramental ministry is not shepherding and pastoring in its fullest sense.

Of course, the apostles themselves were no strangers to the same tension. In the sixth chapter of Acts, they chose deacons, saying, "It is not right for us to neglect the Word of God to serve at table." In fact, the problem they faced was more broadly administrative than time for table service. The broader issue was the proper distribution of the community's goods, and the distribution of limited goods is a quintessentially administrative task. The appointment of the deacons, of course, did not end the oversight of the Church by the apostles and their successors (whether the bishops or their priestly co-workers). The tension can't fully be resolved.

Theoretically, at least, I think St. Benedict has hit on an important insight for holding together the temporal and the spiritual. The two are intertwined. The administration in itself is not simply a distraction. The clearly pastoral and mundanely administrative fit together in a tension that will always remain. Understanding this reality helps, I think, but *living* in that tension for an individual abbot (or priest) isn't entirely resolved by knowing the theory or accepting the insight.

Once again, as for St. Benedict, appropriate delegation is a good response. But, again, like monasteries and probably much more so, delegation in the context of sometimes-complex parish administration cannot resolve the tension between temporal and spiritual duties nor between time for prayer and a very active life of ministry. The challenge of finding a balance in the life of the priest remains even after the interrelation of external responsibilities is acknowledged. In short, the pastor who accepts his administrative tasks and tries to understand them as a part of his ministry must still learn to find a personal balance between his own spiritual life and the many different elements of his ministry.

Pope St. Gregory the Great (540-604)

Enter Pope St. Gregory the Great. Gregory had been a monk and, though perhaps not a Benedictine himself, he was familiar with St. Benedict and his *Rule*, as evident in Gregory's *Dialogues*, the only biographical accounts of St. Benedict.

Gregory was a monk who became pope at a time when the collapse of the Roman Empire in the West left a political vacuum in Italy, leaving the bishop of Rome as one of the few remaining public figures with any authority. In the midst of his great ecclesial and secular responsibilities, Gregory struggled with a certain nostalgia for his old monastic life with its time for prayer and study, its atmosphere of silence conducive to contemplation, and its freedom from the idle chatter that seemed to fill his dealings with secular authorities and persons. He longed *both* to be the bishop that the Church needed him to be *and* a man of prayer and contemplation.

In the end, Gregory came to believe that the challenge for him was to accept and to live in the tension of finding time and energy both for prayer and administration. His resolution is laid out in his classic *Regula Pastoralis* (*Pastoral Care* or *Pastoral Rule*), though elements appear in his other works as well. (We read some of Gregory's reflections each year as part of the Office of Readings in the Liturgy of the Hours.)

Gregory's *Pastoral Care* was the first treatise for pastoral clergy, giving them both practical advice for pastoral ministry but also exhorting them always to live authentically in the tension within which he himself struggled to live—a challenge to bishops and priests as important today as it was 1,400 years ago!

So great are the dangers that accompany the office of bishop and the duties of pastors, says St. Gregory, that no one should accept them if, in good conscience, he could refuse them. Still, Gregory agrees with St. Augustine in praising the lives of contemplatives, but also in maintaining that it would be wrong for a contemplative who was worthy of being entrusted with active ministry for the Church to hold back because of its accompanying trouble and distraction to his prayer.

St. Gregory contrasts the responses of Isaiah and of Jeremiah to God's call. Isaiah responded enthusiastically, "Here I am, send me!" Jeremiah, on the other hand, held back, saying, "I cannot speak..." Here, Gregory sees the tension between embracing the demands of the call while recognizing the cost of living those demands.

But there is no way around the need to balance. Gregory says that the pastor has a duty to speak—instruct, correct, exhort, admonish—but the same pastor must insure that he has something valuable to say. And truly valuable things—offered to the right person at the right time and in the right way—are drawn from the treasury of prayer. All of which is to say that prudent pastoral teaching and decisions (like all true and effective ministry, teaching and preaching) must flow from prayer.

In a similar way, people need the spiritual leadership of bishops and pastors to help them make true spiritual progress. But, asks St. Gregory, how can someone lead others well if he is simply reading a map rather than guiding them along a road that he himself has walked?

Gregory notes the example of St. Paul, who was transported into Paradise and saw things that cannot be spoken (though St. Paul speaks of it as the experience of an unnamed man he once knew). And yet for all the time that such contemplative prayer and experience would have required, St. Paul seems to have left no detail of the life of his churches unattended.

Likewise, Gregory points to the example of Moses, who went in and out of the tabernacle, where he was caught up in communion with God. And yet, at the same time (even with delegation), Moses remained devoted to the affairs of the people. In fact, Gregory suggests that it was in the tabernacle where he communed with God that Moses learned how to respond authentically to the needs of the people.

As these examples show, Gregory followed the common patristic view that both Moses (recall Gregory of Nyssa's mystical treatise *The Life of Moses*) and St. Paul were contemplatives and mystics. But Gregory, in particular, noted that Moses and Paul were both men of deep and consistent prayer *and* leaders with practical concern for their people.

The examples of Moses and Paul point to the life of Jesus, which was full of both very active ministry and very deep prayer. "When Jesus worked miracles in the City," wrote Gregory, "he spent the night in continuous prayer on the mountain." Both/and, not one or the other.

By Pope Gregory's time, the "contemplative life" of prayer had already come to be seen as higher or more perfect than the "active life" of good works and what we today would call "active ministry." But Gregory's own reflection, his prayer, his reading of Scripture, and his own experience and struggles led him to the conclusion that the highest or most perfect form of the Christian life is, in fact, the "mixed life"—the life of prayer *and* active ministry.

St. Gregory has been called the "Doctor of the Mixed Life." It is not the life of cloistered contemplatives that is the highest form of Christian life to which one might aspire. Rather, it is the life of bishops and pastors, well lived in the tension between prayer and ministry. In the mixed life, there is a constant reciprocal movement between prayer and action.

And Today…

Prayer and ministry have to go together. There is no doubt that there is often a tension between them, but that tension must be maintained. A priest has no choice but daily to strive to find a balance.

Prayer empowers ministry—shapes it, directs it, corrects it. But, at the same time, for the shepherd of a community, the ministry—the people and their needs—must regularly be brought into prayer. And by bringing the ministry into prayer, the prayer once again empowers ministry.

Like Moses who learned how to shepherd the people while communing with God in the Tabernacle, the pastor learns in prayer how authentically to lead and minister to his people.

Without regular and sustained prayer, we are left to our own best resources; but as fine and abundant as those resources may be, they are a paltry help to the People of God when compared with the guidance and strength that comes with grace received in prayer.

Without consistent prayer, we are in danger of getting lost in, devoured by or burnt out by the ministry. Without prayer, we are in danger of falling into the idolatry of believing that the real success in ministry depends on us or the danger of being blind to the self-serving that can set into ministry that seeks success as humans account it. Without prayer, instead of the mixed life, we priests can fall into a very mixed-up life.

Surely, Pope St. Gregory the Great was correct in seeing that the bishop, the pastor, the preacher must hold together both lives—prayer and action—so that they can feed one another. Just as surely, he was correct in seeing this lesson in the life and ministry of Jesus, in whose name and person every priest and bishop acts. For St. Gregory, the mixed life, well lived, is the highest and, admittedly, the most difficult.

I am here reminded of an observation of Thomas Merton: Some people look at monks, especially those living a strict observance, and think of the monks' life as heroic. The monastic life appears to them to be a life for the spiritually strong. But, Merton suggests, it is the Christian life lived well *outside* the cloister that is the truly heroic Christian life, the path that requires the real spiritual strength. The monks are the weak ones. They are the ones who need the external rules, the daily scheduling of prayer and work, the regular example and support of others, and even superiors to insure that they are where they should be, to be sure that they aren't accumulating things they don't need, to challenge them to find a balance. The monks are the weak ones who feel the need to be cut off from many of the more crass temptations that surround the average Christian outside the cloister.

If you are looking for spiritual heroes, Merton implies in our context, look to the priests who are striving to be true to the ideal of the mixed life (even if it never occurred to them to call it by that name).

This is the great challenge for priests—to live in the tension without a lot of external supports or enforcement. No one will know if he's not praying his Office. No one will know if he isn't devoting time to personal prayer. No one will know what he's watching on television at night or what Internet sites he visits. None of his parishioners will know; the bishop won't call him in; but it will affect his life and his ministry. Inevitably.

The mixed life is higher or more perfect because it is the more difficult. It requires conviction, commitment, discipline and the development of habits (virtues), struggle (asceticism), support and grace.

But, in the end, how do we hold together our prayer and our ministry, our spiritual-pastoral concerns and the temporal needs of a parish community? How does each priest live this mixed life? When to fit prayer into a busy schedule? How much prayer? What happens when something intrudes? When does prayer time yield to urgent demands of ministry? When does it not yield?

In the end, the answer for each of us must be found in an honest, self-critical discernment (perhaps with a spiritual director or support group) about the actual demands of leadership and ministry in relation to a real commitment to prayer (and to a broader self-care).

Each of us is different in temperament and personality; each ministerial situation is unique, with its own set of demands. There is, unfortunately, no magic formula for finding balance and no final resolution that will not be tested in daily situations and conflicts that inevitably arise.

As in all decisions and apparent conflicts, finding the right balance in the mixed life requires prudence (or "discretion" as St. Benedict would call it) in cooperation with grace. What is certain is that the prudence that will guide us in living authentically each day in this tension is built up by facing one situation after another with a firm commitment to both ministry and prayer. Prudence is acquired by practice; it is a habit. But what is no less certain is the fact that prudence will only be effective if the priest's commitment to his prayer is real. A half-hearted commitment to prayer will inevitably yield in each situation to the task to be accomplished, the phone call to be returned, the person calling for real if not urgent attention.

Martha and Mary

I'd like to conclude with a brief reflection on the Gospel story of Martha and Mary (Lk. 10:36-42). This is, of course, the classic text used to suggest that the contemplative life is the "better part."

Mary is the contemplative, the traditional interpretation goes, who has chosen the better part because she sits and listens to Jesus. Martha represents the active life, and the traditional reading suggests that she has chosen a good, but lesser, way of activity over contemplation. But, really, Jesus chided Martha for being anxious and worried about many things at a time when the presence of Jesus required a different response.

Mary is not praised because she does nothing but sit and listen. Surely, Jesus would not praise her for sitting at His feet in every situation and neglecting important tasks that were hers to do. But at the moment in this story, Martha has allowed herself to focus on good and legitimate activities instead of attending to where the Lord was, what the Lord was saying, and what the Lord was calling her to do at that particular moment. Mary, on the other hand, knew that *now* is not the time for performing the tasks; rather, now is the time for listening, attending to the presence of the Lord and to what He wants. The time for busy activity will come, and, as in Jesus' life, it will require the time for quiet prayer to yield to the responsibilities at hand.

The priest, in this sense, must be both Mary and Martha, both contemplative and active. But, unlike Martha, he must know how to discern what the situation demands, what the Lord requires of him at different times, whether the Lord is present calling him to quiet listening or the Lord is present in a person or situation of need, calling him to action.

In our context, Martha has failed to remain in the tension of the mixed life. She is all activity—good activity, important activity—but she is anxious and worried about many things. So, too, with the dedicated pastor with too much activity and too little prayer—instead of fidelity to the mixed life, he finds his life and priorities simply mixed up.

Conclusion

For St. Benedict, the tension between the abbot's temporal and spiritual duties could be eased by seeing their essential interrelationship (and, ultimately, the priority of the spiritual over the temporal). So, too, for priests.

But the Benedictine abbot at least has external help to maintain the balance at a personal level between his spiritual life and his external responsibilities. He has the demands and rhythm of the common prayer of the community, with set times for personal prayer and *lectio divina*. While he may be as tempted as any monk to take care of some administrative task during the time set aside for personal prayer, at least he has external support.

But, as the former monk Pope St. Gregory realized, the pastor must strive to find that balance for himself with the firm resolve both to prayer and to the work demanded of him. Surely, for the priest of today, the daily Eucharist and the Liturgy of the Hours can provide some secure footing for his personal prayer. Still, it's not easy. At the same, I think it safe to assume that it was not easy for Moses, for Paul, for Jesus, for Gregory or for the countless others who have been called to exercise both spiritual and temporal responsibilities for God's people, responsibilities that must be balanced with their own need for personal prayer and for renewing rest.

Five

Communion and Solitude

People. The daily life of most priests is filled with people and with interactions of various types, at many levels, in a wide variety of circumstances. At the same time, especially as celibates and more likely living by themselves, most priests find themselves alone at least at night, during quickly grabbed meals, early in the morning.

This reality of alternating between being surrounded by people and being alone is not necessarily a tension in itself. At one level, it is simply a continuously changing sequence of seeing people and being alone. It becomes a tension—and *should* become and be *maintained* as a tension—when the priest embraces his identity as a man of communion (which is more than simply a multitude of encounters with people) and, at the same time, fully embraces his need for true solitude (which is more than simply finding himself alone).

True communion is enhanced by true solitude, and a habit of real solitude strengthens the bonds of communion. This is the true tension beyond just the alternating experience of people and aloneness. It is a potentially rich and fruitful tension, but one that is difficult to maintain in actual priestly life and ministry.

St. Benedict has insight to offer for living well in this tension and reaping its fruit. In his *Rule*, he explicitly sets out to describe and legislate a communal form of monastic life, in contrast to the life of hermits. His monks grow in holiness precisely by living the demands of communal living and prayer. And yet, at the same time, the required monastic silence injects a substantial element of solitude into the life of these quintessentially communal Christians. Though lived in markedly different vocations, both the monk and the parish priest must learn to live well in this tension.

Man of Communion

Pope John Paul has frequently spoken of the priest as a man of communion. The priest is in communion with Christ, in whose priesthood he participates in a distinctive way; and through Christ, he is in communion with the Triune God. The priest is in communion with his bishop and with his brother-priests in a diocesan presbyterate. He is in communion with those who collaborate with him in ministry and with the people he leads and serves.

The priest is a man *in* communion. He is also an agent *of* communion. His ministry invites men and women into communion with God, with the Church and with others. He does this, especially and uniquely, through his ministry of preaching and sacrament. Baptism, Eucharist, Reconciliation—really, all of the sacraments—are invitations into communion.

Men of communion, priests are shepherds, pastors, leaders of *community*. They are promoters, gatherers, builders, reconcilers of communities. They are leaders of the community's prayer, especially the Eucharist, which is the heart of the Church's prayer. Even in their private recitation of the Liturgy of the Hours, they are praying with, for and on behalf of the broader community. The leadership and administrative oversight that priests provide is at the service of the community's ongoing life, not simply as an institution but as a living communion of the disciples of Christ.

Priests are heralds of a future—a salvation—that will be communal. Many Catholics can tend to think of heaven in an individualistic way: "me and God." But, of course, it is not. Instead, it will be *all of us* taken up into the very life of God. The Church community, especially at the celebration of the Eucharist, is both a sign and a foretaste of a communal destiny into which priests are constantly inviting their brothers and sisters.

The importance of the Church and of local parishes as community, as well as the important role of the priest as promoter and leader of community, cannot be overemphasized, especially today. Men and women whose authentic human development has been diminished by the individualism of our culture need authentic community life in which to be formed. Men and women living in a materialistic, consumeristic and often-fractured world need to find places of flesh-and-blood, *human* welcome—communities of hospitality in which their uniqueness as human persons is embraced and cherished.

Men and women in a world of confused moral values and skewed moral vision need communities of moral witness, moral vision and values, and moral support to help them live authentic human lives in the world. Christian men and women who want to live faithfully as committed Christians in the midst of the world must find vibrant Christian communities that can pass on the faith to them and support them in living it.

The role of priests as promoters and leaders of community and as those who call others to share their gifts for the life of a community cannot be overemphasized. The importance of their role in building up vibrant communities of welcome and hospitality, of moral vision and values, of faith and celebration, cannot be overstated. But all of this suggests that the priest must himself have a communal vision of his ministry—a vision of his ministry as more than good, one-to-one encounters in counseling settings or passing on doctrine to individuals who happen to be sitting next to each other in the parish hall.

In a particular way, priests must have a special concern for those at the margins of the community: alienated Catholics, marginal Catholics, the poor, the undocumented, those of different ethnic, racial, and linguistic backgrounds. This, too, is an important part of being shepherds and leaders of community. Our ministry must invite and enable them to enjoy full participation in the life of the community.

Communion, community and *people*. A priest's daily life and ministry are full of people—interactions with people of every kind, in different contexts and situations, at various levels of involvement. So central is an ability to interact comfortably and effectively with people that, in the seminary, one of the more common reasons to doubt the presence of a vocation to the priesthood is a lack of adequate social skills. Certainly, the diocesan priest, especially (even recognizing differences of temperament, of introversion and extroversion), must be ready to be a "people person." More than simply possessing the ability to make people feel comfortable or entertained, he must be a man who is eager and able to gather people into communion with God and with one another.

Forming seminarians today for a communal vision of ministry, when the seminarians themselves have grown up in an individualistic society, is a challenge. Helping them to see that priestly ministry involves leading a community, promoting its life and vibrancy, and encouraging its outreach as a community—that it is not only celebrating sacraments, preaching, and offering one-to-one ministry (as important and foundational as these are)—this, too, is a challenge of seminary formation today.

St. Benedict has a great deal to say about community, about what promotes community life and what weakens it. As we have seen, in speaking about the abbot, St. Benedict has a lot to say about how to lead a Christian community effectively. But he and the tradition he fathered also have much to teach about solitude as an important companion to real community life. There is a dynamic tension between the common life of the monks and the solitude created by times and places of silence. I'd like to suggest that to be truly a man of communion, a leader of community, an authentic "people person," the priest must also be a man who can and does embrace an element of solitude in his life.

Man of Solitude

As the Gospels attest, Jesus lived His life and carried on His ministry surrounded by people—crowds of people. More, He was the quintessential man *of* communion and *for* communion. But the Gospel accounts also tell us that His very active involvement with the people co-existed with times of chosen solitude. He went off to pray, unaccompanied even by His disciples. This interweaving of people and solitude is especially evident in this account from the Gospel of Mark (1:32-39 NAB):

> After sunset, as evening drew on, they brought him all who were ill and those possessed by demons. Before long the whole town was gathered outside the door. Those whom he cured, who were variously afflicted were many, and so were the demons he expelled. But he would not permit the demons to speak, because they knew him. Rising early the next morning, he went off to a lonely place in the desert; there he was absorbed in prayer. Simon and his companions managed to track him down, and when they found him, they told him, "Everybody is looking for you!" He said to them: "Let us move on to the neighboring villages so that I may proclaim the good news there also. That is what I came to do." So he went into their synagogues preaching the good news and expelling demons throughout the whole of Galilee.

Like Jesus, the priest must find and live in a fruitful tension between promoting an authentic communion and a true solitude.

Perhaps it is important at this point to distinguish three experiences: being alone, solitude and loneliness.

Being alone is simply a matter of being physically apart from others. It can be experienced positively or negatively. One can choose to be apart or one can find oneself apart. One can enjoy it or hate it. One can be alone physically and yet feel very connected with others through memory. One can use the experience for good or ill.

Solitude, on the other hand, is a chosen aloneness, a choice to be apart from others. Most obviously, solitude can be a decision and an action of being *physically* apart from others; but it is also possible to experience an *inner* solitude, a chosen aloneness even in the midst of a crowd. Perhaps we have all experienced a sense of solitude while sitting at the gate in a busy airport terminal—a sense of choosing to be "apart" for reflection or prayer. In a similar way, driving alone in a car can be an experience of "being alone" with the radio blaring or a real experience of solitude. Being physically separated makes solitude decidedly easier, but true solitude does not necessarily require physical separation.

Some measure of real solitude is essential for the healthy life and effective ministry of priests, for a number of reasons.

Obviously, choosing to be alone provides simple time and space for renewal, physical and emotional. It can help to restore a sense of balance and order to one's busy and hectic life (and a priest's life can easily be busy and hectic).

But there is a kind of private relaxation that is mere distraction and another that is attentive and positive. One can choose to be alone to engage in mindless activity. An evening of watching television is an example of this kind of distraction. Almost all of us have days at the end of which we really want to be passive, do nothing and rest. I don't think that there is anything inherently wrong with such distraction; but, while not bad in itself, it is not very fruitful, and a steady diet of it is numbing rather than life-giving.

There is another kind of relaxation alone that is intentional, attentive, conscious and even self-conscious. It can be, nonetheless, equally relaxing and perhaps even more deeply renewing. Reading, reflecting (as opposed to fretting or problem-solving) and writing are three examples of a more intentional way of being alone.

Solitude—choosing to be alone—allows one to step back, catch one's breath, and put things into perspective. Making time for such solitude and really entering into it can be very difficult on a busy day (or in a series of busy days), full of multiple activities of different kinds with different people in different contexts. But a leader must be able to see the "big picture," to see beyond the mere "fires to be put out." Without some intentional, conscious time in solitude, he may lose his ability to see the whole situation, get lost in the details, or give too much attention to the five percent of the people who quack the loudest. Time apart that is merely mindless distraction doesn't necessarily provide such perspective. It just takes one out of the immediacy of the problem.

But the solitude that I want most to address is a *prayerful* solitude, the solitude that makes deep prayer possible, the solitude that sustained prayer simply requires.

It is in prayerful solitude that the priest renews his personal relationship with Christ in whose person he acts, to whom his life and ministry are meant increasingly to be conformed. The priest is a better shepherd of the people because he takes time away from the immediacy of his important tasks to be alone with the Shepherd whom he represents. And so, in prayerful solitude, he is renewed in who and what he *is*; so that what he *does*, he can do more authentically and, therefore, more effectively.

It is in the solitude of prayer where he communes with God that the priest can form a "contemplative vision" by which he sees Christ in the people to whom and with whom he ministers (even those who are not to his liking). Solitude, paradoxically perhaps, nurtures care for others, because it allows us to see them with the eyes of God. It nurtures a true spirit of attentiveness to others in their need and to their need. Solitude can promote true charity.

Again, perhaps paradoxically, it is the solitude that silence provides within the common life of the monastery that promotes charity. This is reflected in the seeming paradox of hospitality being the charism of men who spend so much time in silence. It is precisely the solitude and silence that promotes the ability to see others as Christ.

St. Meinrad, the ninth-century patron of my monastery, is remembered as both a hermit and as a "martyr of hospitality." He answered a call to be alone, and his solitude formed in him so deep a spirit of hospitality that he died greeting guests whom he knew had come to kill him.

If so with monks, so, too, with priests whose daily ministry can be understood as a kind of hospitality and as an invitation into communion and community.

It is also in the solitude of prayer that the priest forms the contemplative vision—the eyes of faith—by which he can make sense of the sacrifices required by his vocation (that is, his distinctive share in the Cross, precisely as a priest). After all, so much of what a priest does only really makes sense from the perspective of faith. Without regularly renewing that vision, the priest is in danger of judging the sacrifices and challenges—such as celibacy, for example—only from the perspective of human, culture-bound sight.

It is prayerful solitude, then, that sustains the priest in living through the difficulties and challenges, because faith does not have to see beyond every obstacle and every well-conceived-but-foiled plan to trust that the good will be realized, that God will bring the victory, though in His own time and in His own way. In short, solitude is the nursery of hope.

And it is in prayerful solitude—chosen aloneness with God—that the priest can transform the experience of loneliness into a doorway into yet deeper prayer.

Loneliness is the experience of our incompleteness apart from others. We can be lonely while surrounded by others—feel apart from others when we are standing next to them. We can be alone and not lonely at all—not feel apart or separated or distant.

Loneliness, especially in the life of a celibate, can be an invitation to enter into the experience of our human incompleteness and to plumb the depths of our need for God—then, by God's grace and in His time, to discover Him on the other side of our loneliness.

Prayerful solitude can make us, not lonely and emotionally incomplete as priests, but rather, it can contribute to making us more healthy and happy as celibates and therefore more truly available to serve the many.

The loneliness embraced in prayerful solitude can make us cherish others more and make us more ready to reach out to others, especially those who are alone and can make no sense of it.

Thomas Merton believed that it is principally in solitude that a person can cut through the layers of superficiality and falsehood within ourselves to find our truest self—that is, our self as we were formed in the image of God, where we can truly rest in Him and commune with Him (and with other people in Him).

Choosing to be alone with God is not unlike the first Christian monks who went out into the desert to do battle with the demons or like Jesus who went out into the desert to define Himself and His mission. Choosing to be alone with God allows us to confront the "demons" of our own sin—the selfishness, the pettiness, the anger, the fear that keep us from being truly free to give ourselves in loving service.

In order for priestly ministry to be truly self-giving, self-forgetful ministry after the model of Jesus who laid down His life for the flock, we must become increasingly free of motives that are self-serving, self-protecting, self-aggrandizing. Priestly ministry must, after all, be *for them* and not for *me*. Prayerful solitude prepares me to be a better shepherd of others—more concerned for them than for my selfish needs and desires.

Conclusion

The priest is a man of communion, a leader of community, a minister of hospitality. But solitude is a necessary component of his life—as a healthy and balanced human being, as a disciple who trusts in the Lord, and as a priest who must give himself generously in ministry. If he is to be a man of communion to its fullest, he must be a man who holds a time and place for solitude in his life. Solitude enriches his communion and his ministry of communion. Without it, he is in danger of getting lost in the tasks.

Listening for the Lord

Listening to the Word

"...it is the first task of priests as co-workers of the bishops to preach the Gospel of God to all men" (*Presbyterorum Ordinis* 4).

"The priest is first of all a minister of the Word of God" (*Pastores Dabo Vobis* 26).

Clearly, the ministry of the Word—proclamation, preaching, teaching and evangelization as a continuation of and sharing in Christ's own prophetic mission—is at the core of the priest's identity. He is pre-eminently a preacher and a teacher, a prophet in the person of Christ.

Ultimately, of course, all preaching points to the Eucharist, to the paschal mystery of Christ's dying and rising, and to our sharing in it. All preaching points to the Cross present in our lives with its invitation to trust, to surrender, and to see our God present in both the blessed and the unlikely circumstances of our lives. This is why preaching in the context of the Eucharist is its pre-eminent form.

A Challenge for Preachers

At a personal level, to be called to continue the prophetic and teaching ministry of Jesus places great demands on priests in at least two ways: First, the priest must meditate on the Scriptures, becoming more deeply familiar with them and more deeply aware that these sacred texts are the inspired Word of God. Secondly, he must allow the Scriptures to form his own life so that his preaching is never mere words spoken to others, but increasingly apparent in his own living. In short, there must be a growing consistency between what the priest says and how he lives, lest the Gospel message seem non-credible to his hearers.

In the Rite of Ordination for both deacons and priests, the ordinand is exhorted to believe what he reads, to teach what he believes, and to practice what he teaches. In order for the priest to fulfill his vocation as a minister and preacher of God's Word, he must accept that Word himself, meditate on it constantly, have a deep love for it and knowledge of it, allow it to form his own life, and let it shine out in his daily living.

"Let them remember," say the Council Fathers in *Dei Verbum* (25), "that prayer should accompany the reading of sacred scripture, so that a dialogue takes place between God and man." This challenge directed to all Christians carries particular weight for the preachers of the Word, whose ministry must be firmly grounded in prayer with the Scriptures.

In a similar way, the Congregation for the Clergy (*Priest* 202-3), teaches: "Effective preaching is another fruit of personal prayer." Effective preaching comes from a prayerful encounter with the Lord who wills to speak to His people, so that authentic preaching grounded in prayer has power to reveal God's Word to these particular people in their need at this moment. The authentic preacher, then, who would continue the prophetic and teaching ministry of Jesus, must be a man of prayer. And so, in *Pastores Dabo Vobis* (26), Pope John Paul teaches:

> ...The priest himself ought first of all to develop a great personal familiarity with the word of God. Knowledge of its linguistic or exegetical aspects, though certainly necessary, is not enough. He needs to approach the word with a docile and prayerful heart, so that it may deeply penetrate his thoughts and feelings and bring about a new outlook in him—the "mind of Christ" (1 Cor. 2:16)—such that his words and his choices and attitudes may become ever more a reflection, a proclamation and a witness to the Gospel. Only if he "abides" in the word will the priest become a perfect disciple of the Lord.

True Preachers of the Word, True Hearers of the Word

To be proclaimers and preachers of the Word—in speech and in witness—we must first be true *hearers* of the Word. We must hear not only with our *physical* ears but, as St. Benedict says in the first verse of the Prologue to his *Rule*, with the "ear of your heart" (RB Prol.1).

If what we are to proclaim, preach and teach is to be the Word of God and not just our well-educated and well-intentioned musings, perhaps eloquently delivered, we must listen, and we must truly hear. Only then can we hope to preach God's Word and not our own.

If all that we do is study and think about the Scripture texts and figure out "the message" or the "theme"—or, worse, simply depend on "homily helps" (which can have their place) without even much personal engagement with the texts—the resulting homily might make some good and interesting points, but it will remain the fine thoughts of a mere human being, rather than God's Word for these particular people at this particular time. And what a sparse meal that would be to offer the People of God, who have come to be fed by God and not by mortals, no matter how learned or clever!

The Word of God is never merely a generic or abstract word that is meant to "fit" all people in all circumstances in exactly the same way—"one size fits all." God's Word, proclaimed and preached, is always a Word for particular, unique people and communities (which is why the same Sunday texts can legitimately yield a countless variety of different emphases and interpretations in the homilies preached in the churches throughout the world on any given Sunday—similar phrases and themes brought together in an endless variety of ways by different preachers for different communities). The Word of God is always a word *for me*, for *this* community, to break open our little world, our mundane corner of human existence.

To break open God's Word—as we often speak of preaching—we must allow ourselves to be broken open by it. In their document on the Sunday homily, *Fulfilled in Your Hearing* (pp. 20-1), the Bishops' Committee on Priestly Life and

Ministry teaches that preaching is not so much interpreting the Scriptures; rather, it is interpreting our lives in light of the Scriptures.

Probably, most priests have read the *Lectionary* texts in preparation for the Sunday homily and thought, "Now, what am I going to say about *that*?" But, of course, this is really the wrong question. The right question is, "What does *God* want to say to me and to these people to whom I am sent to preach His Word?"

The Word of God is always a word for me and for my life—for this community and our life—in our current circumstances. But, sometimes, I suspect that we priests are just a little too sophisticated, too well educated, or too dependent on commentaries (as valuable, even essential, as they can be) to truly believe that simple truth.

Often perhaps, our faith is not simple enough to sit down with a biblical text and pray quite simply (after reading the learned commentaries to gain insight into the text): "Lord, what do You want to say to me and the people in this passage?"

Or sometimes, we are too busy to take the time to calm down and be quiet enough to hear a word from the Lord that might come to us. It's just easier for the distracted mind to read the commentaries, think about the "point" of the text, and prepare the homily from there.

Or perhaps, at times, we don't really want to believe that God's Word is a word for me, because we are afraid of the demands that God might make on us. And for sinners like us, what scriptural text does not have its demands? What might

God ask me to do? What might He ask me to surrender? What challenge would He have me speak to these people—some of whom won't want to hear it?

In a number of languages, the word "listen" is closely related to the word "obedience." Certainly, obedience requires listening. We can't be obedient to God's Word and to His will if we aren't willing to listen; and if we aren't ready to submit to that will, then we have ample reason, conscious or not, to close "the ear of our hearts."

St. Benedict: Listen!

What does St. Benedict have to say to contemporary preachers? Well, directly and explicitly about preaching, not much; but he and his spiritual tradition have a great deal to say about listening to and praying about God's will revealed in the Scriptures.

The Rule of St. Benedict opens with the invitation and the challenge: Listen! The *Rule* then goes on to describe a way of life filled with the Scriptures: the communal recitation and singing of the psalms, canticles, and Bible texts, as well as the private reading of the Scriptures. It presents a daily schedule in which hours are set aside for holy reading and the silence necessary truly to listen and to hear. The text of the *Rule* itself is full of quotations and paraphrases from the Bible, as well as scriptural allusions. It is apparent that its writer was both intimately familiar with God's Word and desired the same for his monks.

In many ways, the monastic life described by St. Benedict is very different indeed from the busy life of a contemporary priest. But, at the same time, the priest's life, too, is filled with the Scriptures: daily Mass readings and homily preparation; the psalms, canticles, and readings of the Liturgy of the Hours; and Scripture briefly shared with parishioners in a variety of contexts. And, for the priest whose "first task" is to preach the Gospel, there is a more urgent reason for him to heed St. Benedict's challenge to listen: His prayerful attention to God's Word is not only for himself; it is so that he can authentically and effectively proclaim and preach God's Word to His holy people!

Lectio Divina

Over the centuries, there developed in Benedictine spirituality a kind of "method" for meditating on the Scriptures and other spiritual texts called *lectio divina* ("holy reading"). It is a tool to enable us to respond to St. Benedict's challenge to listen and thereby truly to encounter God in His Holy Word. For the priest, who is first of all a minister of God's Word, this proven tool for biblical meditation offers help to insure that it is truly *God's* word, rather than his own, that he preaches to the people. Then, listening for the voice of the Lord each day in prayerful encounter with the Scriptures, the priest is better able to listen to the Lord throughout the day—in his decision-making, in interacting with parishioners and staff, in finding balance in the midst of the many and varied activities of a priest's day.

Lectio divina is not just another name for spiritual reading, the attentive reading of spiritual books. It is an attitude toward, an approach to, and even a technique for a deep engagement with the text and with the One who speaks there a word for the priest and for his people.

Traditionally, there are understood to be four steps or movements in *lectio divina*: *lectio* (reading), *meditatio* (meditation), *oratio* (prayer), and *contemplatio* (contemplation). Here, I can offer only a brief summary of these steps, but I would begin by noting the time-honored, practical and essential advice about preparing for real prayer: find a quiet place; breathe deeply; relax; say a prayer for the grace to pray well. Because *lectio* is about listening, it is critical to take time to slow down and to quiet down.

Lectio

Today, we are so used to reading for quick information: newspapers, magazines, memos and reports, and e-mail (scan it and then delete it!). Usually, we are reading just slowly and attentively enough to get the basic message.

Lectio—actually reading the biblical text—requires a different approach. Recall that the medievals had no printed texts, and manuscripts were precious and scarce. In those days, even when reading privately, people read aloud, softly. Monks in particular would read a text over and over again, committing parts to memory. It is no surprise, then, that the *Rule* is filled with words and phrases straight from the Scriptures, as was the case with so many patristic and monastic texts. St. Benedict's scriptural quotations and allusions came from his memory as he wrote, not from a check of his handy concordance later.

In *lectio*, the person at prayer reads the text slowly, over and over again, allowing himself to notice words, phrases and images that catch his attention. It is on this page that God will speak to him. At this point, he is neither really thinking about the text nor responding to it in prayer. He is, rather, listening, attending and trying to remain open.

Meditatio

In this second step, one begins to reflect on the text, to engage it actively, by asking oneself questions about it and its meaning, especially those phrases and words that have caught one's attention. Here, scholarly or popular commentaries can be helpful to understand the passage in context and its meaning to its original readers. (Of course, many of us can find these commentaries interesting, and there is an abundance of fascinating research and interpretation, but we must avoid the temptation to use up our prayer-time in studying the commentaries. Focused biblical study can take place at another time.)

Clearly, this is more "active" meditation, in the traditional sense. While one can mull over the text, one can also imagine oneself as part of the scene. What might the Lord be saying to me and to my community in this word from His inspired Word?

Oratio

The person praying over the biblical passage now responds in active prayer. The reader questions God or responds to a perceived message or asks for guidance, forgiveness or strength in light of the challenge offered by the text. One enters more deeply into the prayerful encounter with God as He is present in the text by responding to it and to Him in prayer. By responding actively from one's own experience, the passage is accepted more deeply as a word to me, rather than a text to be pondered abstractly or merely intellectually, calling for no personal response.

In my own prayer, I have used a prayer journal to record my prayer response to the text. As part of the *meditatio*, I will often write down the verse, the phrase, or the word that has struck me. Sometimes, I will read a commentary. Then, in the journal, as part of the *oratio*, I write the prayer that I make in response to God. For me, the practice of writing keeps me from merely thinking about the text or making my prayer-response perfunctory, and it keeps me focused.

Contemplatio

This final stage, of silent attentiveness and listening, is often —and easiest—to neglect. Yet, it is the most important. Although one has already thought about the message that God may have for me in the text and responded in prayer, now is the time to shut up and listen. And that's the really hard part! I may discover in quietly listening at that moment—or later in the day, as a word or phrase comes to consciousness—that what I *thought* God had to say to me in the text is not what *listening* ultimately and more accurately revealed to me.

A tool for keeping focused and internally quiet at this stage is the silent repetition of one of the words or phrases that garnered one's attention upon first reading. The point here is not to think about the phrase or reflect on it; the point is just to repeat the word as a kind of mantra to slow one's breathing, to push away distractions, and to stay quietly focused. Here, *lectio* meets or can lead into centering prayer.

By grace, this active practice or repetition can open one to a truly wordless resting in God, where no explicit message at all is revealed and no word is spoken, but God speaks more truly, wordlessly, silently, heart-to-heart. And this is the goal of all praying, to rest and commune with God.

Obviously, *lectio divina* takes time and, on certain blessed days, can stretch on. Probably, about half an hour is a good amount of time to set aside. *Lectio* also requires us to commit ourselves to slow down enough to do it daily, to try to put out of our minds the thousand things that run through them. (The point, remember, is listening; and we have to turn off the internal cacophony to do it.) Like all prayer, sometimes the experience is rich and sweet; at other times, it is as dry as bones. Personally, I commit myself to sit down in my chair and, whether full of consolation or seeming desolation, I will not rise from that chair for the allotted amount of time. When I find my mind wandering, I refocus. If the experience is dry and boring, I tell myself that I am going to sit there anyway for the allotted time. As spiritual masters have said, dry prayer is in some ways really the best prayer, because it is time and effort devoted to God without the selfish benefit of consolations.

Conclusion

The practice of *lectio divina* is meant to form a deeper spirit of listening during one's prayer times, but also in one's life outside those times. It is a method that can help to prepare a particular homily, but I am suggesting that *lectio* as a regular, daily prayer practice is not really, simply or even primarily for preparing to preach a particular homily. Rather, as a habitual way of praying, it can form in the preacher a deeper respect for the Word of God, a deeper trust that God is present and speaking in each and every text, and a more consistent and reliable attentiveness to Him at every moment and in every ministerial situation.

Priests have a special relationship with the Word of God. We are privileged to proclaim and preach that Word, and so we have a special responsibility to "enter into" the Word and allow it to enter into us. St. Benedict's challenge to listen and the practice of *lectio divina*, more particularly, can assist us in doing precisely what we must do as priests: Accept God's Word; receive it with joy; meditate on it constantly; be nourished by it daily; believe it; practice it; teach it; and proclaim it in word and in action.

Seven

A Spiritual Program for Listening

Obedience, silence and humility—these are the topics of chapters five, six and seven of the *Rule of St. Benedict*: Chapter Five on obedience, Chapter Six on silence (*taciturnitas*, perhaps otherwise translated as "restraint of speech"), and Chapter Seven on humility.

Many commentators on the *Rule* suggest that these three chapters and these three topics form the heart of St. Benedict's spiritual teaching. In fact, in speaking of any one of the three, St. Benedict seems always to speak of the other two. In any case, it is obvious that, in the mind and in the teaching of St. Benedict, these three—obedience, silence and humility—are intertwined and, together, are central to the life of the monk.

I would like to suggest that these three (even though they sound very much like the special concern of monks) have much to say to the life and ministry of priests as well.

Tools for Listening

It seems to me that much of what St. Benedict is talking about in these three chapters points back, in turn, to the opening injunction of the *Rule*: Listen! "Listen carefully, my son…." Listen to the Master and, ultimately, listen for the Lord. Listen to the voice of the Lord as He calls out each day. "If you hear his voice today," St. Benedict reminds us, "do not harden your hearts." Attend as the Lord calls out and speaks. Silence, obedience and humility, in the end, are all tools for such listening (and, of course, readiness to act).

Silence

Silence (or "restraint of speech") provides the external and internal conditions to listen and, therefore, to hear. *External* silence is, of course, a tool for the *true* value, which is an *interior* silence. The outward silence provides a context for an inward silence—though the former is no guarantee of the latter. Someone can refrain from speech, but be full of an internal cacophony.

Silence is a leaving behind, or putting aside, or perhaps a tearing away of the noisy clutter that surrounds us and that comes to fill us. In silence, we get behind the noise that insulates us or distracts us or hides us from the word that our Lord wants to speak. Silence is for listening.

St. Benedict's challenge to promote space for silence in our lives is as important today as it was then (perhaps more so) and as important for busy priests as it is for monks (and, again, perhaps more so). You and I live in a noisy world, some of which is beyond our power to change, but much of which is sadly of our own making (or at least the result of our own complicity). How many of us, after all, live in a world in which the radio or the television or the cell phone is rarely turned off? Wake up in the morning, and turn on the radio or the television (or both). Get in the car and turn on the radio. The last thing to do at night: turn off the television and/or the radio.

While it's true that much of the noise in the heart of our day goes inescapably with the busy ministry of priests in a complex society, what I'm really talking about are the times in which a little quiet is possible, but we avoid it: in the early morning before the hectic pace of the day begins (instead of the chatty interviews of morning television news shows), late at night (instead of the late-night talk show hosts), in our cars, in the office during the day between appointments or meetings.

A lot of the noise of the world lives inside of us, and we allow it to live inside of us. In fact, all too often, we cultivate the noise. And we do so, because at some level, we don't *really* want to hear the Lord's word to us. Our lives, as complex and mixed up as they can be, are comfortable as they are. God's word can be so challenging: forgive people we don't want to forgive, let go of things we don't want to let go of, give away what we don't want to give away, spend more time doing *some* things when I have a lot of other things that I need and want to do.

We don't *really* want to hear; and so, when we do try to set aside time to listen, it is so very hard to cut through the noise. And, of course, we blame God that we find ourselves so distracted, that quiet prayer is so difficult, and that we can never seem to hear God's voice so that we can know His will. "Speak, Lord, your servant is listening…at least if what You have to say is something I want to hear…or at least if it won't upset my world too much…or at least if it's a message I can hear just after having turned off the radio!"

Silence is for listening. But it only works if really you want to hear.

A priest must be a proclaimer, a teacher, a preacher of God's Word. He must speak the Word of God to the people. But how can he speak God's Word, rather than merely his own human-and-tainted-by-sin word or opinion, if he is not a true hearer of that Word? And how can the priest be a hearer if he is not a listener? And how can he listen unless he is willing to cultivate silence in his life—an interior space to hear the voice of God? How can a priest truly be a proclaimer and a teacher and a preacher—or, for that matter, a man of prayer and a true disciple—if he allows his every waking moment to be filled with noise from outside and from within?

Without silence, the priest is in danger of being just another motivational speaker or a clever orator or a purveyor of pious platitudes who has learned the vocabulary of faith. But a priest without silence cannot truly speak God's Word for the lives of these people who need and deserve to hear God's Word, rather than be shortchanged by hearing merely the best pious thoughts of this inwardly noisy priest.

Obedience

Silence is for listening. But it only works if you want to hear.

True silence, then, already implies obedience. The one who is truly silent is open to listen and ready to hear. And to be truly ready to hear is itself already an openness and even a willingness to change—to change at least my viewpoint or my opinion and perhaps even my way of thinking and therefore my way of acting and perhaps my way of being. Obedience is simply the last moment of truly listening.

Obedience, for the monk, means trying to listen for God's will for him—most typically through the needs of the community. Sometimes, the monk will discover God's will through the mouth of the one called by God to discern those needs on behalf of the community. A monk accepts an assignment in a spirit of ready obedience, because he accepts that God has called the abbot to discern and to direct the community according to its true needs. But St. Benedict also speaks of "mutual obedience" (RB 71), through which the monk listens for God in the words, the example, and the immediate needs of his brothers.

Sometimes (hopefully, most often), such obedience will come easily for the monk, whether because the task is light or agreeable or because the monk has allowed grace to make him docile. But sometimes, such obedience will be difficult, seemingly hard and impossible (RB 68). Obedience, even then, forms in the monk an even greater docility to God's will rather than to his own.

Silence and listening and hearing and obedience, then, require trust—trust that God *wants* to speak a word to me, trust that God *has* a particular will for me, trust that God's will for me is always good even if I cannot yet *see* its goodness for me, trust that God *does* speak through some whom He calls to a special leadership, trust that my obedience even to a mistaken judgment by another will make me a better listener and a less self-willed disciple, trust that God will make a better good come from my obedience even if the abbot's direction is wrong-headed.

Every priest makes a promise of obedience; and such obedience, when difficult or seemingly wrong-headed, can make him, too, a better disciple and more free of his sinful self. But the priest's obedience is not, in the first instance, a tool for his personal spiritual growth (though it can be), nor is it merely a tool for efficient management of a complex ecclesial organization (though it can be). The priest's obedience is for mission. His obedience is for the sake of the mission to which he surrendered himself on the day of his ordination, a mission that he acknowledged is not his own but undertaken under his bishop and with his brother-priests.

His gifts, his talents, his plans, his projects, his priorities were surrendered for the sake of the mission. If it were *his* mission given to him personally and privately from God, he could follow his own best lights. But it is not *his* mission. It is a shared mission given by Christ to the Church under the authoritative leadership of his bishop, to whom he has promised obedience for the sake of that mission. And, in carrying out that mission with his brothers in the presbyterate, perhaps we can speak (as St. Benedict does to his monks) of a "mutual obedience," as the priest seeks to be, not a lone ranger, but a collaborator with his brother-priests and their lay collaborators in ministry.

A Deeper Obedience

But it seems to me that there is yet another kind of obedience, a deeper obedience, in life. There is yet another kind of willingness to listen and to hear and to be changed.

What shall we call it? Obedience to life as we find it? Obedience to the cards we've been dealt in life? Obedience to the Cross—to the necessity of the Cross, the inevitability of the Cross, the painful truth that there is no salvation, no faith, no discipleship without the Cross?

It seems to me that when silence, obedience and humility come together in a listening heart, the heart open and anxious to hear, the heart ready to be docile, then and only then, a person can accept the suffering that cannot be taken away, the burden that must simply be carried, the injustice that, for now, cannot be righted. Then, one can accept the Cross, and the listening heart can hear the voice of God—even there, even then—saying: Trust! Accept! Surrender! Embrace the Cross as your path to holiness, your being conformed to Jesus, your roadway to sanctity!

That, it seems to me, is true humility, true obedience and true discipleship as a follower of Jesus. And it can only be realized in a heart that has cultivated silence in order to listen, to hear, to trust and to surrender. Otherwise, the suffering is just senseless suffering, the burden is just an arbitrary burden, the injustice is just life's capricious unfairness—and the only response, then, is anger or bitterness or frustration or self-pity or escape in the countless ways that human beings can seek escape.

Suffering can teach us a deeper obedience. Suffering can teach us a truer humility. Suffering can invite us into the silence in which we can hear the Lord say, "I am with you—even here, even now. Trust in me! Accept! Surrender!"

What shall we call it? Obedience to life as we find it? Obedience to the cards we've been dealt in life? Obedience to the Cross? Whatever we call it, it is the only true path of discipleship, the only sure road to sanctity.

Humility

It seems to me that humility is the attitude of one who listens and who stands ready to obey.

Humility is the attitude of one who knows that what he needs most is something he himself does not possess, and so he must listen and wait on another. Humility is an acknowledgment of dependence.

The humble person listens because he knows that the word—the word of forgiveness, the word of acceptance, the word of love, the word to guide and direct his life, the word that he most needs to hear—is a word that cannot come from himself. And ultimately, it cannot come from any other creature.

Humility is the attitude of the creature—the sinner—who stands in awe before the One whose love alone can embrace the sinner, cleanse him, and make him divine through a sharing in the divine life.

Humility is the attitude of one who has already surrendered and stands ready to surrender yet again.

Priestly Humility

Priesthood, of course, is a type of leadership in the person and in the name of Christ the Head and Shepherd of the

Church. The Church is hierarchical. Authority and power are tools for leadership in the Church. Priests, even when appropriately collaborative, hold such authority and wield such power.

And because this is so—because priests are leaders who hold authority and wield power—they need a healthy dose of real humility. Humility reminds the priest of what he is and what he is not as he stands in the place of Christ at the head of His people.

Most fundamentally, humility reminds the priest that "God is God, and I am not." It is almost nonsensical even to say it, but it is a reminder that priests need to hear from time to time (as silly as it sounds in the saying). If God is God, and I am not, then I can be free to give over the effort and the final determination of success to Him. And, if God is God, and I am not, then my first task is to listen to what *He* wants in the multiple ways that He will tell me what He wants (whether through prayer or through the voice of the bishop or through the advice of brother-priests or through the counsel of fellow ministers, parish leaders, and the People of God themselves). If God is God, and I am not, then my attitude ought to be remembrance of that reality, some silence to listen to what God wants to say or wants me to do, and a readiness to obey (even if the message I get is not the one I want to hear).

Humility reminds the priest that "Jesus Christ is the savior, and I am not" or, in its more liberating form, "Jesus Christ is the savior, so I don't have to be." Humility allows a priest to leave the saving up to Christ. All I have to do is my little part (which is usually challenge enough!).

Every priest is ordained to share in a distinctive way in the priestly, prophetic and kingly mission of Christ—distinct from the way that all of the baptized share in His office as priest, prophet and king. The priest's unique calling is a special gift. In fact, it is an awesome wonder: a sinner called to share in the priesthood of Jesus Christ in a distinctive way.

But the more the distinctiveness, the greater the need for humility.

The priest is ordained to share in Christ's *prophetic* role in a distinctive way. Humility, then, must teach the *prophet* that he must first listen before he presumes to speak, because the word that the true prophet speaks is the Lord's word and not his own. Humility teaches the *teachers* that they, too, must first—and continuously—learn, because the Truth to be taught is the Lord Himself and the truths that He wants imparted to others. In fact, in the mysterious and wonderful things of God and ways of God, true teachers will always be learners—or they will never truly be authentic teachers. Humility teaches the *evangelizers* that they must first and always be themselves more deeply evangelized, more deeply converted, if their lives are to be consistent with and empowering of the words they speak.

The ordained priest participates in the *priesthood* of Jesus Christ in a distinctive way, allowing him to mediate, to sanctify, to reconcile, and to offer sacrifice, as others cannot. What an awesome privilege and wondrous vocation! But humility, then, must remind the mediator, the sanctifier, the reconciler that the self-offering that must be united with that of Christ is not *only* the self-offering of the people but also his own.

Humility reminds the priest that there are depths and dimensions and aspects of his own life desperately in need of sanctification—in fact, more in need of sanctification precisely because he is himself a minister of holy things and holy actions. Humility reminds the reconciler that it is his own sin, too, that must be reconciled. It reminds the ministers of reconciliation that no one needs ongoing reconciliation more than they. (And so, the humble priest knows that he needs regularly to celebrate the Sacrament of Reconciliation *as a penitent* if he is to celebrate it worthily and well as its minister.)

The priest stands in the place of Christ at the head of His people, sharing distinctively in His mission as *Head, Shepherd and Pastor*. Humility, then, must remind these would-be pastors that they themselves are always in need of guidance. They are limited and weak and in need of co-workers and collaborators. They, too, stand under other shepherds, for the sake of a shared mission to which they have surrendered themselves and which is not their own personal, private possession. They, too, stray and need to be brought back. They, too, sometimes need to be carried. They need the pastoral care of others.

That Love Which Casts Out Fear

St. Benedict concludes Chapter Seven, on humility, by assuring the monk that faithfully following the way of humility (and therefore, implicitly but necessarily, silence and obedience) will lead him to "that perfect love of God which casts out fear" (RB 7:67, citing 1 John 4:18).

How is it so? How does humility (and silence and obedience) lead to a perfect love of God that casts out fear?

I believe that sin is ultimately rooted in fear. Sin arises because we are seeking after things (other than God) to make us feel secure, safe, in control, independent. Some people seek after possessions, others after power, others after human respect, and still others after proofs of sexual attractiveness and even conquest. But, of course, none of these things can make us secure, safe, really in control. Rather, these things gain control over us so that we always want more—need more—possessions or power or human respect.

In the end, it is only by trusting in God, only by surrendering to Him and to His loving will, only by allowing ourselves to be held in the safety of His embrace, that we find peace, security, safety, fulfillment. This is the truth that Jesus, surrendered to the Father on the Cross, taught us most definitively.

Humility—and silence and obedience—leads to the perfect love of God that casts out fear. Silence provides the context for listening, humility is the attitude of the one ready to hear, obedience is the readiness to surrender to the Word once heard.

The person who allows himself to be silent before the Lord, who is humble before Him, and ready to be obedient to Him is truly surrendered to Him. Such a person has laid aside the false things that can never make him secure, safe or authentically independent. Such a person has recognized his need for the Lord, for His mercy, His love and His strength; he has listened and heard that word of divine love; he has surrendered to it;

and he trusts in it, no matter the happy or the tragic events around him. And so he has no need for fear; fear no longer has power over him, tempting him to grasp after anything that is not God.

He knows himself loved; he has surrendered to that love and to the certainty of its triumph; and he has given himself—that is, loved—in return. Humility and silence and obedience have led him to that love of God that casts out fear.

Such surrender is the goal of *every* Christian life. It is by no means unique to monks or priests. All of us must unite ourselves with Christ and offer ourselves to the Father with Him. This self-offering is what makes all of the baptized participants in the priesthood of Jesus Christ. But it is the special and unique tasks of ordained priests to promote, nurture and guide this priestly self-offering of the priestly People of God. Priests do so in a unique way at the Eucharist, in which they stand in the place of Christ and gather the self-offering of the people so that Christ can gather them into His own self-offering to the Father.

But this work is really carried out throughout the ministry of the ordained—helping their brothers and sisters to surrender to God at critical moments in their lives and in the everyday, in joy and in sorrow, in new life and living, and in dying, in praying and in deciding. Surrender to the Father after the model of Jesus—and the truest peace to be found only there—this is where silence, obedience and humility are meant to lead.

Conclusion

Silence, obedience and humility have their own distinctive forms in the life of monks. But what Christian can come to true peace, to that love that casts out fear, to holiness—except by embracing one's need for the Lord, by learning to find quiet before the Lord so that one can listen to Him (whether to be comforted or challenged), and by standing ready to surrender to Him whatever the circumstance?

Silence, obedience and humility must find a place in the life of every Christian. They must find a *distinctive* place in the distinctive life and ministry of priests if they are to serve the priestly surrender of the priestly People of God.

Listen and surrender! We must teach that message to the people, but we must struggle faithfully to live it first ourselves.

Seeking an Ordinary Holiness

Eight

Spirituality of the Ordinary

When we're young, we tend to be full of high, even naïve, ideals, dreams, and "great expectations." In general, no one faults the young for such idealism—nor should they.

When we're young in age and in the spiritual life, we tend to have high, even naïve, ideals about the life of the Spirit, the attainment of sanctity, and prayer. We say things to ourselves like: "Okay, I've *really* decided to be a man of prayer. *This* time, I *really* mean it. That *last* time, I must not have been serious enough. By next week, I'll be spending an hour in *real* contemplative prayer; and, by the week after that, I'll be having visions."

Maybe we read a little biography of St. John of the Cross or a beautifully poetic passage from one of his mystical works, and we decided that we were ready to start the ascent up the slope of the mystical Mount Carmel.

Or maybe we read a pious biography of another saint and had dreams of being a great missionary. We decided that we would dedicate our entire lives to working with the poorest of the poor. Or maybe we decided to be the humblest of the humble, pious and gently loving to everyone we meet. "People will notice," we would tell ourselves in our naïve zeal. "They'll say, 'Boy, have *you* changed!'" (If not by next week, then by the week after that.)

Of course, as we get older, in age and in the spiritual life, we realize that it isn't quite that easy—and it isn't likely to get that way. We find that prayer takes effort and, for long periods, it can be as dry as dust. In fact, it can be a struggle. It can *often* be a struggle. "*That* time" that we were "*really*" going to make prayer a real priority—"*that* time" has become many, many times.

It's true that the life of St. John of the Cross was heroic. His poetry is sublime. But actually trying to read *The Ascent of Mount Carmel* is tough going—much less trying to *live* its doctrine. It is a mighty steep climb from the foot of Mount Carmel to the "*nada, nada, nada*" at the summit.

My grand plan was to become an instant pious and gentle saint—well, the people around me *did* think that I seemed happy (or maybe just a little odd) for a few days, but I soon fell back into old patterns. (One time, for several days, while in my young naiveté, I felt a sustained sense of recollection and relatively effortless prayer. And my friends *did* notice a difference in me. They asked me if I was depressed.)

And, despite my grand vision of myself as a hero to the poor, the first time I really worked with the poor, I discovered that they were just people—some of them courageous, grateful, faith-filled; others manipulative, dirty, bitter. Of course, work with and for the poor is noble work, but there's not much romantic in the doing of it.

Of course, the aging process itself serves to temper a good deal of our naïve idealism. Mid-life, in particular, teaches us a lot of lessons. By middle age, our romantic ideals have bashed up against brick walls enough, we've "lived in our own skin" long enough, to know that many of our lofty goals are just not going to happen as quickly or exactly as we would have liked or expected. Life is what it is. I am what I am. The people around me are as they are.

In face of this realization, we are left with at least two possible roads to walk, two options.

The first option is cynicism. My naïve ideals won't bend or adjust in the face of the less-than-ideal life as I actually live it and observe it around me. The ideals remain in their lofty heights, but no one (including myself) lives them—or *can* live them. So, we are left disappointed, cynical and perhaps bitter.

Cynicism is one sad, and sometimes ugly, form of high and naïve ideals unrealized. And, sadly, most of us probably know priests who are cynical about everything: initiatives undertaken by other pastors, efforts by fellow priests at spiritual renewal, and ideas of parishioners for new evangelization or parish revitalization.

But there is another possible response to the confrontation of ideals with the reality of human life as we find it in others and ourselves. That other road is acceptance—not the abandonment of our ideals altogether, but a tempering of them, a "reality check."

The second response isn't an abandonment of the path on which our ideals have set us, but an acceptance of the fact that it's just going to be harder and take longer than we had thought. The heights of Mount Carmel *can be* scaled, but it's going to take one step at a time (and a heart kept open to the essential empowerment of grace).

Such acceptance—such idealism tempered by realism—leads, not to complacency, but to peace. You can still read the pious biographies of saints (I do), but you read them with a different eye—not a cynical eye, but with an appreciation of both the heroic example of saints and realistic appraisal of their humanity and our own.

When many fellows come to the seminary (or the monastery), they tend to be wide-eyed and even a little starry-eyed. They arrive and find themselves surrounded by like-minded, faith-filled and generous fellows. They love the camaraderie, the "brotherhood," the community. Daily prayer, daily Eucharist—what a treasure! And the seminary faculty and formation staff—saints! So attentive, so approachable, and such obvious men of prayer!

Then, by week three, they've discovered that some of the guys around them don't seem as pious as they had seemed. Being expected at Morning Prayer *every* morning—even after a late night of research and writing—isn't always the pure joy it once seemed. Some of the priests on the seminary staff have some quirks. And, by week five, these novice seminarians wake up to the fact that they themselves aren't holy yet. They're still struggling with the same old sins, having trouble praying, etc. And it occurs to them that maybe this seminary idea wasn't so good after all.

This, and moments like it throughout seminary formation, are critical, as the seminarian comes to a sense of acceptance that balances ideals and common human reality: "The people around me haven't arrived yet…and that's okay. I haven't arrived yet…and that's okay, too. It's okay with me, and it's okay with God."

It seems to me that there are three "acceptances" to which we must come: We must come to accept *others* as they are; we must accept ourselves as *we* are; and we must believe that *God* accepts both them and us. It seems to me that if we could do any of one these perfectly, we could do them all.

The successful resolution of these crises when idealism encounters reality is an essential moment in formation for what will come in the future. In the seminary, of course, we are attempting to prepare seminarians for priestly life as it really is, with all of its challenges and difficulties, even while we are trying to instill its ideal—priestly life, as it *ought* to be lived.

Of course, when our graduates leave us, they are still young—if not in years, at least in priestly life. And no matter what we tell them, some of them leave feeling that all of the people will love them; they'll have no conflict; they'll spend ten hours preparing each Sunday homily—for which the people will be oh-so-grateful; their still-slightly-shaky prayer life will suddenly find solid ground; their commitment to the Liturgy of the Hours will remain unshaken in the more unpredictable life of the parish; celibacy will be no problem; and obedience will be a snap.

But those graduates soon discover that *none* of it is that easy —the prayer, the preaching, the pastor, the people and the staff. Celibacy, too, can be a lot harder to live when you're alone in the rectory, feeling a little unappreciated, than it was in the seminary when friends were available down the hall.

Eventually, idealism must be tempered by realism. But what of the universal call to holiness spoken of by the Second Vatican Council? What of Pope John Paul's call for priests who are not only effective but also holy—indeed, more truly effective *because* they are holy?

Priests hear so many calls to be men of prayer, so many challenges to *total* self-giving in priestly ministry, so many exhortations to priestly holiness! And, surely, no priest can disagree with the appropriateness of these challenges, for themselves and others. But how to *live* the challenge? How to make their ideals a reality in our ordinary human existence?

Enter St. Benedict. Benedict wanted nothing less than holiness for his monks. His ideals were no less lofty. But St. Benedict believed that authentic spirituality is lived and true holiness is attained in the ordinary circumstances of our lives: in the rhythm of prayer and in the mundane service of others. The daily bearing of the burdens of others (and patiently bearing the burden that others sometimes are to us), the ordinary living of the vocation—sticking to it, staying with it, being true to it in the ups and downs of our lives. All of this—and nothing more heroic or extraordinary—is St. Benedict's path to holiness. And it is a good path for priests and, indeed, for every Christian.

The late medieval monastic reformer St. Bernard called the monastery a "school of charity." It sounds lovely and idealistic. But he also said that life in community is one of life's greatest penances. In fact, the two statements make perfect sense in relation to one another. The monks learn love of neighbor and a real love of God by bearing patiently and living generously, one day after another with a bunch of other sinners. Authentic love is learned in the ordinary circumstances of the "school of charity" by bearing the penance that others are to us.

Expecting the monk to find holiness in the ordinary living of one's vocation, for St. Benedict, *fidelity* is critical. And so, the monks vow both *conversatio morum* (ongoing conversion) and stability (sticking to it in *this* place with *these* people).

This path "works," St. Benedict implies, if we are faithful to it, mindful of it (intentional about it), and even zealous about it. And it is not easy. Such prolonged, daily fidelity, mindfulness, and resolve isn't easy. But it is very ordinary.

I think of the cure of Naaman the Syrian in the Second Book of Kings (5:1-27). Naaman was a great general of the King of Aram, but he was a leper. In desperation, he went to Elisha the prophet seeking a cure. But Elisha was unimpressed with the arrival of the great man, accompanied by chariots, soldiers and extravagant gifts. Elisha simply sent out word, "Go down and wash seven times in the Jordan."

All of it was just too ordinary for Naaman. He was expecting great invocations and a grand waving of hands. But to wash in the Jordan? It was all too ordinary, but it was precisely in the ordinary that the great leader of armies was healed.

Isn't that a message of the Incarnation? Isn't that a message of the birth of the Savior of the World in a humble manger? Isn't it the message of the God-made-flesh who ministered and prayed, who ate and laughed and cried, who had friends and who was busy with many things but found time to be alone on the mountaintop?

In the monastic tradition, one of the great enemies of the monk's life and prayer is *acedia*, the "noon-day devil." When the path to holiness is fidelity to the ordinary tasks of one's vocation, one important enemy is a kind of boredom, a dissatisfied distraction that tempts the monk to look vainly outside the usual and the mundane. And so, the monk, sitting in his cell, one day after another, gets restless. He thinks, "Probably, Father Paphnutius needs help. I should walk over to check it out." Or he thinks, "This is too mundane. Surely, there's something more spiritually extraordinary that I should be doing or someone with whom I could be talking about holy things."

The prescribed traditional remedy for *acedia*, this restless spirit? Shut up. Go back to your cell. Do what you're supposed to be doing. Weave your basket, and recite your Psalter.

What would most priests say to a sincere married couple who asked about the pursuit of holiness in their married life? Would we say to them, "No hope for that! Your lives are too ordinary!" or "Well, okay, live like brother and sister, quit your jobs so you can pray for several hours a day...."

No, we'd say, "Wonderful! Of course, it won't be easy! It will take time for prayer. And finding—and making—that kind of time available in a busy day will be hard, especially if you have kids. You'll have to be both dedicated and realistic about it."

Then, we'd go on to say something like, "But, for the rest, you'll find your holiness in your daily self-giving: in being faithful to your marriage through difficult times and temptations, in being attentive to one another and your children, in being generous with your time and energy, in being willing to sacrifice and to forgive, etc."

Isn't that what we priests would say to a sincere married couple who wanted to pursue holiness? It might seem all-too-ordinary, but, surely, we all believe that real sanctity for them would be found in embracing their vocation faithfully, generously and prayerfully.

If this is the answer for the laity, why do priests expect something else for themselves? Isn't a priest's holiness to be found, most basically, in being faithful, mindful, and dedicated to his vocation and its day-to-day demands?

It might not be extraordinary nor seem all that heroic, but don't we all know how difficult such fidelity really is, one day after another?

In fact, the path to priestly holiness is lived in daily fidelity to prayer in the midst of many important tasks and competing demands on one's time. It is lived in fidelity to the struggle to grow in prayer, even as one struggles to become more faithful to the authentic demands of the ministry.

The path to a priestly sanctity is found in faithfulness to the daily effort to carry out our obligations generously and well—whether sacramental, administrative or pastoral. It is found in maneuvering the reasonable and sometimes-unreasonable burden that our obligations are to us—with a minimum of sustained whining, complaining or self-pity.

A priest's holiness is found in the ordinary, but challenging, effort to be generous with the people he encounters in the daily course of his ministry: patient with those who irritate him, forgiving with those who offend or oppose him, rising above his discomfort with conflict where a situation requires it, and rejoicing in those who love us in our flawed humanity, inspire us, or make us laugh (especially at ourselves).

Priestly holiness is found by living faithfully in the tension: between prayer and active ministry, between pastoral and administrative tasks, between serving others and finding solitude for oneself, between self-giving and appropriate self-care.

A priest's sanctity is found *in the midst*—in the midst of prayer, daily Mass(es), meetings, visits to the hospital, dinners, exercise, memos and mail, appointments, homily preparation, and more meetings. In the midst of it all and not separate from any of it.

Extraordinary? No. Ordinary, but perhaps heroic in daily fidelity to it all.

I was struck when I first read a paragraph in the Congregation for the Clergy's *Directory for Priests* that challenges each priest to view his presbyterate as the "place of his sanctification." It sounds, to a Benedictine, like the vow of stability. Priests are always ordained to a particular flesh-and-blood presbyterate. *These* priests—saints and sinners alike—in *their* diocese—are the context of the priest's path to holiness.

Whatever bishop comes, whatever the next generation of priests looks like (whether liberal or conservative, U.S.- or foreign-born), however the diocese and the demands of priestly ministry changes, whatever future assignments a priest might receive, this particular diocesan presbyterate is the "place of his sanctification." By staying with these brother-priests and those to follow them, the priest will find his holiness.

Surely, within every presbyterate there have been, and hopefully are, priests who are considered holy by their brothers. Sometimes, this opinion arises because of some heroic virtue or some obvious sanctity. But probably more typically, these priests are considered to be holy precisely because they have been faithful, and they have found peace in being faithful. Their fidelity has been marked by humility, generosity, perseverance and hope (which we know, from experience, can only mean that prayer has remained an important, if hidden, part of their lives).

If we sincerely consider such "ordinary" fidelity in another obviously flawed human being to be one indication of real sanctity, why do so many priests look for a different kind of holiness? Why do they hold themselves to some other, more exacting, standard?

Other priests and lay men and women, we all agree, attain their sanctity in faithfully living their vocations in the ordinary, mixed-up, complex circumstances of everyday life. Perhaps it is easy to believe, with St. Benedict, that monks are to find holiness in a faithful living of prayer and work in the context of a community of fellow sinners. Why would a priest look for a different path to attain his own holiness?

Surely, there are heroic priests whose virtue and sanctity merit official canonization. But, for most of us, St. Benedict's expectation of attaining holiness through a spirituality of the ordinary is just as surely a real sanctity, nonetheless.

In the end, for the vast majority of us, where else would we look for the holiness to which we believe we are called, both as Christians and particularly as priests? Our Lord has called us to a distinctive vocation in the real world as we find it—with its own particular responsibilities, burdens and blessings. He has called us to holiness within that vocation. Even if it is true that our present circumstances are not the most felicitous for aiding us on our journey, shall we assume instead that the universal call of holiness doesn't really apply to us? In the end, isn't looking for an alien holiness (that is, outside of life as we actually find it) either an invitation to leave our vocations and commitments or to find an excuse not to take up the hard work that real holiness requires for every vocation? Isn't the latter option really a "cop-out"?

What constitutes the "ordinary" circumstances of the lay, the clerical and the monastic vocations are certainly different. But, surely, St. Benedict is right to insist that all of us must look for our holiness in the midst of the life to which we have been called and in which we find ourselves.

For those of us who have been tempted to despair of attaining the spiritual goals of our youth, St. Benedict's message offers renewed hope. To those of us who have found excuses to avoid the acceptance of the daily, hard work of sanctity in the mundane, he offers a challenge to take up our starry-eyed ideals once again, but with a greater wisdom gained through age and experience.

Nine

Willing the One Thing

In its 1994 *Directory for the Life and Ministry of Priests* (citing both the Code of Canon Law and Vatican II), the Congregation for the Clergy challenges priests in this way:

> The priest, although not having assumed poverty as a public promise, must lead a simple life and avoid anything which could have an air of vanity, voluntarily embracing poverty to follow Christ more closely. In all aspects (living quarters, means of transportation, vacations, etc.), the priest must eliminate any kind of affectation and luxury (*Directory* 67).

In fact, both the *Decree on the Training of Priests* (*Optatam Totius* 9) and the *Decree on the Ministry and Life of Priests* (*Presbyterorum Ordinis* 17) of the Second Vatican Council emphasize the need for priests and seminarians to embrace and to witness a simplicity of life. Pope John Paul reiterates the teaching in *Pastores Dabo Vobis* (30), and it finds a place in the U.S. Bishops' *Program of Priestly Formation* (297-98).

In all of these documents, voluntary poverty—and a broader simplicity of life—is consistently exhorted for a wide variety of interrelated reasons. I will summarize some of these in "bullet points":

• Through a voluntary poverty, the priest is more *free*—in a practical and human way—to move, as necessary, to meet the needs of the Church. (One can assume that a priest would be more reluctant to accept a transfer if he knows that it requires a couple of vans to move all of his stuff—with the added fear that he has many valuable things that could get broken or lost in transit.)

• In a related way, I think we can see a priestly simplicity of life as part of a broader sense of *balance* in a priest's life—a balance that can be hard to attain in the light of the many demands and responsibilities of priestly life and ministry today. Life is complex and cluttered enough without adding the clutter of many possessions.

• Practicing simplicity of life—having what one reasonably needs and little more—the priest is better able to practice good *stewardship* over earthly goods. This is important for the priest, both in his personal life and in his related stewardship over the goods of the Church for which he has pastoral responsibility.

• Through simplicity of life, the priest *imitates Christ*, "who became poor that we might become rich." Jesus' life gave testimony that what he needed, he received from the Father.

• Like Jesus, in voluntary poverty, the priest stands more clearly in solidarity with the poor and the marginalized.

• Not only does the priest thereby give witness to others, the priest is thereby better able to approach the poor as one who can be seen as sympathetic to their situation. He is better able to speak *to* the poor and *for* the poor in a more credible way.

• The priest, through a simple lifestyle, gives witness in a world in which materialism and consumerism often skew the human sense of what is important in life.

• And, at its heart, simplicity of life represents an interior freedom from which a real selflessness can flow. The unnecessary accumulation of material things can suggest an inner neediness, as if material things could provide a security that they cannot.

It is really this "interior freedom" on which I want to focus my attention. Such freedom is the human foundation for a true imitation of Jesus in the way of poverty and simplicity.

St. Benedict on Private Ownership

Benedictine monks traditionally have not vowed "poverty," strictly speaking, but rather "community of goods" (which is why medieval Benedictine monasteries could accumulate large estates. The individual monks may not have owned anything, but the community could have vast holdings. Abuse of this understanding of poverty is one of the reasons for the reaction of the mendicants—friars—with their emphasis on radical poverty, individual *and* communal.).

But, in fact, St. Benedict was against—almost fanatically against—private ownership by the monks. Instead, the monks should mirror the life of the post-Resurrection community recorded in the Book of Acts (4:32-34), in which all things were held in common. Depending on the monastery for all of his temporal needs reminds the monk of his ultimate dependence on God. And, as long as he has what he needs—

no more, no less—there is less chance for envy, which can be so divisive in a community. Today we say, "If you want peace, work for justice." In a real way, St. Benedict was saying, "If an abbot wants peace, root out private ownership, which is the cause of envy and divisions."

My abbot, Archabbot Lambert, is certainly an excellent example of voluntary poverty. When we moved into our "new" monastery in the hot, humid summer of 1982, I was assigned—after helping the elderly and infirm monks move their things—to move the possessions of then-Father Lambert, who was away at the time. I thought to myself, "Now, here's a real pain. He's not even here, and I'm going to have move a huge pile of his stuff." (And, believe me, it was a hot and humid August in that old, un-air-conditioned monastery!)

But when I got to Father Lambert's cell, I thought that someone had gotten there ahead of me. Because, in fact, besides whatever he had taken with him on his trip, he had one small and very light suitcase, one suit bag, and one small cardboard box. Period. That was it. Even today, the Archabbot says that he could move out of the abbot's quarters in minutes. And I believe it!

St. Benedict wanted to see such poverty in his monks, ultimately as a sign and as a path to a deeper spiritual poverty. Real poverty—real simplicity of life—is grounded in and promotes an interior freedom—a freedom from grasping. In the monastic tradition, this is called purity of heart. Purity of heart is the abiding attitude, the interior disposition, of one who is free from such grasping and clinging.

Sin Rooted in Grasping

As I mentioned in a previous chapter, it seems that the root of all sinning is fear (and fear leads to grasping after things that are not God). Sin is grounded in the misguided, misdirected, and ultimately tragic effort to protect ourselves. The unnecessary accumulation of things—and the envy of those who possess more than we do—is just one manifestation of this skewed self-protective venture (and probably not its worst form). The effort to attain a real simplicity of life—voluntary poverty—is just one avenue to root out sin in our hearts more generally.

Adam and Eve had the "good life" in the Garden. God walked with them in the cool of the day. He cared for them and provided everything they needed. But, then, the serpent came along and said to them *not*, "Rebel against God." "Scorn Him." "Become His rivals."

No, the serpent was far more subtle. He said, "Look how dependent you are! You are so needy, limited and contingent (as we might say). Eat of the Tree of the Knowledge of Good and Evil, and you will be like gods (that is, you will be the source of your own security, autonomous, independent, safe in yourselves)."

But what the serpent suggested was a lie. For there is no safety, no security, no comfort apart from God and from what He provides. But after Adam and Eve had bought the lie and reached out for that forbidden fruit, their children throughout the ages have grasped after some*thing* to make them feel secure, safe in themselves, not dependent. We have continued to live and to perpetuate the lie.

The children of Adam and Eve grasp after material things—as if the accumulation of passing, superficial things could make them safe or secure or ultimately happy. It's a trap—like an addiction. You always need more things to try to feel secure; but since they never really work, you always need even more.

Voluntary poverty is the effort to let go of a prop that can never work anyway. It is the effort to break the endless cycle of accumulating more and more—and better and better—things.

Of course, for many of us monks and priests, forgoing the collection of material things would be the easy thing to do (relatively speaking), because most of us are grasping after more subtle and satisfying ways to feel secure. (After all, you don't generally go into the monastery or into the priesthood if the possession of material goods is your chief way of trying to feel secure apart from God.)

Instead of material things to make ourselves feel secure, autonomous, independent, many of us are grasping after what has traditionally been called "human respect." We grasp after the praise and respect and admiration of other people, as if that would make us secure or happy. But, of course, a little praise or occasional human respect is never enough. It becomes addictive. It enslaves our freedom. We need more and more.

In fact, St. Benedict cuts to the core of this temptation—this form of the lie—by warning his monks not to allow themselves to be called holy until they are. To seek to be called holy is, after all, the height of seeking after human respect for us religious types. Of course, if you really were holy, you'd be too humble to admit it (or too humble to see it), and you certainly wouldn't want or need anyone to acknowledge it.

Seeking after human respect is a "good" alternative to seeking after things—a more subtle and less crass way to try to feel secure, safe, independent apart from God. But there are still others: titles and high office and power—all of them addictive and all of them false. In themselves, they are all good things—just like material things and respect and seeking after holiness are good things in themselves. But the temptation for the children of Adam and Eve is to grasp after these things as if titles or high office or power could really make them secure, safe, or independent of God—any more than material things can.

But none of them works. None of them. Not one.

Only in God are we secure. Only in God are we safe. Only by recognizing and accepting and living in our complete dependence on Him can we discover the truth and be free.

Dependence, trust, surrender, acceptance, abandonment, obedience, poverty, simplicity—the words that, in all honesty, make our skin crawl because they are the exact opposite of the lie that we have been taught to believe—are some of the words that express the deepest reality of our existence and the only path to true security and peace.

This is a lesson that Jesus taught us most perfectly. This is why "he became poor that we might become rich."

Hanging upon the Cross—unjustly condemned, betrayed, ridiculed, alone—He refused to call down angels. He refused to lash out at others. He refused to grasp after any*thing* to make Him secure.

Jesus, on the Cross, did what no child of Adam and Eve had ever done before: He just trusted. He surrendered. He accepted. He abandoned Himself. He obeyed.

In life and upon the Cross, Jesus was poor—poor with a deep and profound poverty that made Him truly free and that now should mark the lives of disciples, and most especially His priests.

Voluntary poverty—simplicity of life—is just one part, one small step, in developing the true poverty of spirit that acknowledges our complete dependence on God.

The One Desire

Born into a world of sin—a world of grasping after security in things, in human respect, in titles and high office, and power—yet, deep within each of us, there is the desire for one thing—the one thing necessary.

Deep within each and every human heart is the desire for God—for communion with Him—for life within His heart.

In all desiring, it is Him whom we desire.

But our many desires become misguided—things, human respect, titles, status and power—rather than God—as if there could possibly be ultimate comfort or satisfaction or security in any of them.

And so, we come to St. Augustine's classic definition of sin: *aversio a deo per conversionem ad creaturas* (turning away from God and turning toward a created good…as ultimate end…as a source of ultimate security).

Purity of Heart

St. Benedict (following Cassian, the desert monastic tradition, and the post-apostolic fathers) exhorts his monks to *purity of heart*—what, in another tradition, might be called poverty of spirit.

The purified heart is *not* a heart "purified" of desire, passion or love. The purified heart is the heart in which desires are ordered, passion is integrated, and love is directed, not to self, but to God.

To be pure of heart is to be single-hearted. The pure heart is the undivided heart. It is the liberated heart.

The meaning of purity of heart is captured well by a title of a collection of essays by philosopher Soren Kierkegaard: *Purity of Heart is to Will the One Thing.*

Purity of heart is to desire one thing, to be passionate for one thing, to will one thing—and to will anything and everything else in light of the one thing necessary: God and communion with Him. God and God alone

Of course, the pure heart is poor. It clings to nothing other than God. It wants nothing other than God. It is free.

In the Life of Priests

Priests are exhorted to live and to find their distinctive holiness in pastoral charity—in selfless self-giving for the flock entrusted to them—after the model of Jesus who came to serve, not to be served, who laid down His life for the sheep. It is the pastor's self-forgetful love for the flock that empowers his ministry, that integrates the variety of tasks that a shepherd's ministry requires, that leads him to holiness through the pouring out of his life for others.

(I'm not talking about heroics here—I'm talking about the daily generosity, the hard work, the sacrifice, the other-directedness that daily ministry requires—alongside the many joys and the rewards and the blessings!)

But we will not—we cannot—truly, consistently, completely give ourselves in ministry as long as we are grasping after anything other than God for our security. We cannot, at one and the same time, be seeking things or human respect or title or status or power and *really* give ourselves in ministry.

Real charity requires a purified heart—a heart free to love, to give itself.

Real *pastoral* charity, giving oneself in ministry and in authentic priestly leadership, requires purity of heart—a heart free to love, to give itself.

If we are ever to become truly good and authentic and even holy priests, then, with the lifelong struggle it takes and with the mighty help of God, we must purify our hearts. We must allow *God* to purify our hearts.

To love as a pastor should, we must desire the one thing. We must have a passion—yearn for—the one thing. We must will the one thing.

And, we must give up grasping after anything that is not God—whether something as obvious as material things or as subtle as power. We must do this for the sake of our own authentic spiritual growth, but, as priests, we must do it for the people who look to our example and who have the right to receive good example from priests about what is truly important in life. How can we preach that the Lord must be central in their lives and that they must always trust in Him—how can we preach that message to them when it seems obvious that God may be *important* in our lives but hardly *central*? How can we preach trust, when anyone can see how we cling to our own superficial props (whatever they may be for each of us)?

Patristic and monastic authors taught that the deepest prayer requires a foundation in purity of heart. Only the heart focused on Him, only the heart yearning for Him, only the heart willing communion with Him—trusting Him, surrendered to Him, abandoned to Him, obedient to Him—only such a heart could truly be open to receive Him, truly and deeply, as fertile ground for the deepest prayer.

Surely, truly deep prayer is not meant to be the exclusive goal of monks. Even in the very different circumstances of the life and ministry of priests, such deep attention to and communion with the Lord must be a realistic and a real goal. Otherwise, how will the priest most authentically speak God's word and act in the person of Christ? Otherwise, how will the priest attain the holiness to which he is most certainly called? But, as we have seen, deep prayer requires a heart that wills the one thing.

Conclusion

What a task! What a challenge! What conversion must lie ahead!

What would it take to attain such purity of heart? Well, grace, of course; an uncompromising self-critical eye; the frank observations of spiritual directors, confessors and true friends; asceticism ("struggle"—struggle against the grasping we find in our hearts); openness to be reminded of our complete dependence on God and nothing else, as we encounter the Cross that no human action can take away; and actually embracing the Cross of surrender and trust and abandonment when it is thrust upon us. And, again, at the end as at the beginning and throughout, grace—the grace that comes from prayer and the sacraments, the grace that is all around and fills us with riches beyond measure, if we will just open our hearts to receive it.

Ten

Continual Conversion

As a moral theologian—before I became more absorbed in seminary administration—I was very interested in the relationship of spirituality and ethics, between our moral lives and our spiritual lives, our lives of virtue and of prayer. I had come to believe, along with many other moral theologians, that our discipline was too exclusively focused on solving individual moral dilemmas (as important as that project is), and we were not spending enough time either re-reading the moral wisdom of St. Thomas Aquinas or taking up the challenge of the Second Vatican Council to make moral theology "shed light upon the exalted vocation of the faithful in Christ and their obligation to bring forth fruit in charity for the life of the world" (*Optatam Totius* 16).

At the same time, as a man struggling to grow in prayer myself—to be faithful to prayer and to deepen my prayer—my experience was already telling me that prayer can't be sustained and grow unless, at the same time, one's daily living is becoming more consistent with the ideals and practice of one's prayer.

Looking to traditional Catholic spiritual theology taught me that, before you can profitably read *mystical* theology, you have to absorb *ascetical* theology. I learned that our tradition had always taught that, to get to the top of mystical Mount Carmel, you actually have to climb its sometimes very steep slopes. In short, there is no being "airlifted" to the heights of prayer (except perhaps by some miraculous and apparently rare divine intervention).

With those discoveries in reading and in experience, I became suspicious of what we might call "cheap" spirituality. In other words, I became suspicious of books on *techniques* of prayer that seem to suggest that, if you simply follow a particular prayer-method, you can attain the heights of prayer (as if those lofty heights can be scaled without a deep and consistent change in one's daily living).

I became doubtful about teachings on prayer that seek to provide good *feelings* in prayer—which is fine in itself *unless* it leaves you there, because feelings in prayer are notoriously passing and unreliable. If you want to know if you are having "good" prayer, our tradition tells us, don't examine your feelings. Rather, see if your prayer—whether sweet in its consolation or bitter in its dryness—is bearing fruit in greater virtue, in greater charity. You know the health of the tree by the fruit it bears.

I became suspicious, not of charismatic prayer in itself, but of emotional, affective prayer without moral change.

I became suspicious *not* of centering prayer in itself. (In fact, centering prayer is a great tool, and, as I have said, it can fit well with the "*contemplatio*" step of the Benedictine practice of *lectio divina*.) But I did become suspicious of implications that centering prayer could make you a contemplative—when I had learned that contemplation grows only in the soil of a virtuous life.

I re-discovered for myself the Three Ways—the identification of three stages in the spiritual life—really, in the Christian life in general: purgation/purification, illumination, union.

From at least the third century, our spiritual tradition spoke of these Three Ways. In fact, the Christian life has *always* been seen as a process; a progression, a dynamic—a path, a way, a road, a journey, a pilgrimage, climbing a mountain, running a race or (for St. Benedict) ascending a ladder.

In short, the Christian life is a way of *conversion*—moral and spiritual, virtue and prayer, both/and—a way of *holistic* conversion.

Pope John Paul's addition of the Luminous Mysteries of the Rosary serves to fill out our meditation on the life of Jesus, the unfolding story of our redemption. But the new mystery with which I am most happy is the "Proclamation of the Kingdom of God and the Call to Conversion": "This is the time of fulfillment. The Kingdom of God is at hand. Repent and believe in the Gospel."

With the introduction of this new mystery, we will meditate regularly on the call to conversion. And, while it may sound like a call, an invitation, and a challenge that was made only *once*, by our meditation on this call regularly, it may jar us into really seeing it and taking it up as a daily renewed challenge: *Now* is the time! Repent!

Conversatio Morum

One of the distinct vows taken by a Benedictine is the vow of *conversatio morum*. I remember a great deal of emphasis in my novitiate class on the *Rule of St. Benedict* that the correct Latin word is *conversatio* (which implies a dynamic, ongoing, continual quality) rather than *conversio* (which would suggest a more static, one-time conversion).

The Benedictine vow of *conversatio morum* is a vow of continual conversion of the monk's ways to the monastic way of life. It is a vow continually to take on, more deeply and more completely, the identity of a monk—becoming more what one has been called to be and vowed oneself to be.

Our novitiate at Saint Meinrad is still (relatively speaking) pretty traditional: special permission to leave the monastery grounds; no personal money; no private telephone, television, or Internet connections; limited family visits; permissions required to visit, for any length of time, with the seminarians; required common recreation; and required manual and menial labor.

The novitiate is supposed to pull a fellow out of his old life and plop him down squarely in a new one. It's for that reason that I can understand (and appreciate) monks who say, "Novitiate was the *hardest* year of my life." I think, "Well, good. That means you had to change, and changing can hurt." On the other hand, I wonder when another monk says, "Novitiate was the *happiest* year of my life." I think, "Did it pull you out of your old life or not?"

At the end of a year of novitiate, yanked out of his old life, the young monk takes his first vows, including the vow of *conversatio morum*—the ongoing conversion of his life to the monastic way of life. Then, by living the monastic life faithfully, one day after another—doing his assigned work without grumbling, being faithful to personal and communal prayer, bearing with his brothers, doing his *lectio*, keeping silence, listening to his superiors, learning from the good example of his seniors (and accepting the reality of bad example, too)—by doing these things and by picking himself up when he has failed to do them, he will become more authentically a monk. He will become, gradually and over time, what he professed himself to be at the beginning because he believed that's what God called him to be.

How will these things more authentically form him as a monk and lead him through continual conversion? Doing these things faithfully—one day after another, through the good days and bad, when he wants to and when he doesn't want to—that consistent fidelity to his vocation will lead him through conversion by teaching him self-forgetfulness, by teaching him surrender, in short, by requiring him daily to take up the Cross.

And, in the end, is there really any other tool for authentic growth in the Christian life? Does conversion happen any other way? Is there any other instrument—other than the Cross daily embraced—that leads to real holiness in any state of life?

What does it mean to obey a superior for the good of the community—when you'd rather not, when you have other plans, when you reckon that another course of action would be better?

What does it mean to serve the other monks—when you don't feel like it, when you know that their service next week will not be so diligent as yours, when you don't particularly like this particular brother whom you are serving?

What does it mean to bear with the burdens of others patiently—bear with the burdens that some of these monks seem to *be*—when it's the same old burden that you've been putting up with for years?

What does it mean to do work well that you don't want to do—without grumbling, without complaint?

What does humility mean? What does obedience mean? What does service mean?

In the end, aren't they all forms of self-giving, self-forgetfulness, self-gift?

Isn't it, in the end, all about taking up the Cross of one's vocation—and allowing *that* Cross daily to kill what is false, root out what is sinful, reveal-in-order-to-exorcise what is selfish, self-serving, self-directed?

What authentic Christian path is there that doesn't mean *daily* taking up the Cross in the form that you find it in your vocation?

This, it seems to me, is the path of ongoing conversion. Whatever the vocation—whatever form its Cross takes—can there be any other path to real Christian conversion?

Chapter 72 of the *Rule of St. Benedict* is on the "good zeal" of monks, and there he says,

> This, then, is the good zeal which monks must foster with fervent love: *They should each try to be the first to show respect to the other* (Rom 12:10), supporting with the greatest patience one another's weaknesses of body or behavior, and earnestly competing in obedience to one another. No one is to pursue what he judges better for himself, but instead, what he judges better for someone else.

Be the first, says St. Benedict, to show respect *to the other*. Support in patience the weakness *of the other*. Obey *the other*. Pursue what serves better *for the other*.

It sounds sweet in the reading. It is the Cross in the actual living. And, for the monk, it is the path of ongoing conversion.

The path of conversion, then, can be an arduous one. How difficult it is to take up the Cross—and especially to do it daily, one day after another. It is asceticism—that is, it involves struggle.

But, thanks be to God, God is good. He is so good.

In our lives as monks, He gives us so much joy, so much goodness, so much for which to be grateful, so much to sweeten, to balance, to lighten the Cross: like-minded confreres (*some* of whom are funny, supportive and inspiring), the quiet beauty of the liturgy, the sense of a Godly task, good work on behalf of the Church, guests who are so grateful for our way of life, yearly celebrations that have the character of family by their uniqueness to us, and so many more things....

God gives us so much to lighten the Cross, to help us to carry it, or (to put it another way) "with every vocation, comes the grace to live it."

Seminarians

I think seminarians should take a vow of *conversatio morum*—the daily conversion of their ways as they are formed for the priesthood. In a way, of course, they do. It's called Admission to Candidacy—when a seminarian commits himself publicly to continue diligently his priestly formation.

Every seminarian should live a vow of ongoing conversion by daily embracing his formation in all of its breadth and facets. He should give himself over to his studies—not because he particularly likes this or that particular class, but because even the class that he finds the most uninteresting is preparing him to be the best possible priest (a priest who will undoubtedly find some aspects of ministry uninteresting to him and even burdensome).

A seminarian should live his vow of ongoing conversion by praying the Liturgy of the Hours and his personal prayer every darn day whether he feels like it or not, whether he feels he has time for it or not—and maybe most especially when he *doesn't* feel like it and when he feels he *doesn't* have time for it. And one reason he should do so is to fortify himself for the day when the busyness and the complexity and the routine of priestly ministry will tempt him to think that he is too busy for prayer, or can get by without it, or that he can survive as a healthy-but-prayerless priest—spiritually empty to the point that he only rarely *feels* like praying at all—maybe as he notices the God-given beauty of a fall day and then quickly rushes to the next darn thing.

A seminarian should live a vow of continual conversion by generously serving others in the seminary community, even though it might be inconvenient to him, by embracing chastity in his viewing of television and movies and Internet sites even though our society would tell him that he is being prudish or scrupulous; in short, by embracing the Cross as he finds it in his seminary formation. Because the Cross is the only sure path to the conversion that will form a man into a dedicated and effective and holy priest (and if a man feels called to be a priest, what other kind of a priest could he want to be?).

The Priest

And, of course, I think every *priest*, too, should take a vow of *conversatio morum*. In fact, of course, he does—on the day of his ordination when he gives himself totally to God and to the Church. The daily challenge for the priest is to conform his ways to the priestly way of life, to the way of life of the True Shepherd in whose priesthood he participates.

The priest must strive to become daily more what ordination has already made him: specially configured to Christ; specially configured to Christ the Shepherd who guides and provides care *and* who laid down His life for the sheep; specially configured to Christ the Head who governs and leads *and* who came to serve, not to *be* served; specially configured to Christ the King who reigns now in triumph but whose earthly throne was the Cross on which He laid down His life; specially configured to Christ the Prophet, the Teacher, the Evangelizer who announced the Kingdom and taught us its ways *and* who did so by His living and by His dying and His rising. This is the path of his priestly conversion: to become what ordination has made him through the daily tasks that his vocation lays before him each day.

The ongoing conversion of the priest's life involves letting the challenges of his life make him more deeply and thoroughly what he already is—just less and less of him (his false, sinful self) and more and more of Christ. In this, St. John the Baptist is the exemplar: "He must increase; I must decrease." I must become increasingly like Him and less like my old sinful self—until I can say with St. Paul, "I live now, not I, but Christ lives in me."

What is the path of our ongoing conversion—whatever our state of life—but all of the things, great and small, that require us to surrender ourselves—and, as priests, to forget ourselves so that others can remember Him?

There are, for all of us, those great times of struggle, challenge and doubt. But the surrender that is the path of our conversion is most usually found in the more mundane invitations to give of ourselves: our precious time given to someone we don't know or don't like or who approaches at an inconvenient time, our presence when we would rather be elsewhere, a decision that is right but that will bring us hardship, a message that needs to be spoken to people who don't want to hear it, attention given to God when the television or the task to be completed seems more appealing or more urgent. Each is an invitation to surrender, to give and to die to self. But where else is a disciple of the One who surrendered on the Cross to find a path to true discipleship and to an authentic holiness? How else does a man specially configured to the Priest who offered Himself as the Victim on the altar of the Cross become more truly what his call and ordination have made him to be?

The path of priestly conversion involves struggle, but…thanks be to God that God is good! Thanks be to God that God is so good to His priests! Thanks be to God that He sweetens the Cross, that He gives joy to balance the affliction: the awesome wonder of a priestly call, the joy of a sublime mission, the support of brother-priests and fellow ministers, the privilege of presiding at the sacraments, of being welcomed into the homes and sometimes-fragile lives of good people, of preaching God's Holy Word.

And, through it all, the Lord is there to help—His grace, His patience, His acceptance of our frail humanity, His forgiveness when we fail and when we fall, His constant and ever-renewed call to conversion—to pick up and try again.

Conclusion

Of course, this work of conversion is never complete in this life. One theologian suggests that we should see conversion, not in a linear way, as if we were moving along a line, never to pass the same point again. But, rather, we should see conversion as a spiral—re-visiting the old issues, the places in need of healing, the roots of our selfishness at different levels, at different times, with slightly (or very) different lenses.

The lesson of the vow of *conversatio morum* is: "Become more consistently, more deeply, more completely what you are called to be, what you committed yourself to be, what you already are!"

As a Christian disciple, become a more docile, teachable, disciple. As a Christian, become a clearer, more authentic reflection of Christ—draw closer to Him, become more conformed to Him, love more truly as He loves. As a seminarian, become more intently, more wholeheartedly, more consistently one who is allowing himself and making himself to be formed to be a dedicated and effective and a holy priest. And, as a priest, become more transparently Christ the Shepherd in whose priesthood you participate, in whose place you stand, in whose name and person you act, whose people you are blessed to lead and to serve.

Such ongoing conversion is fueled by gratitude. The Christian who ponders the Good News that God loves sinners—that God loves *this* sinner—finds reason for wonder, reason for gratitude, *and* reason to take up the path that roots out sin and allows him or her to respond to the gratuitous love offered by God.

And the priest who daily ponders the awesome wonder of his call—to what ministry God has called this sinful creature—such a priest finds cause for wonder, cause for gratitude, cause for daily taking up the task of being conformed more truly to what God has so graciously, so wondrously, so undeservedly called this sinner to be!